Foreword

Pastor Lee embodies the ministry of an armorbearer. He has lived that message for over three decades as a part of the founding team of Victory Life Church. He has served the body of Christ with a loyal and pure heart without wavering.

Armorbearers were essential to leaders throughout Scripture. Life or death, in many battles, was in the hands of this trusted defender of their commander. The leader's success or failure was directly connected to his armorbearer. Those on the front lines in ministry today are not so much in physical battles, but rather spiritual ones. Many pastors and leaders are failing for a lack of loyal and faithful people around them. Every pastor needs armorbearers to fight the good fight of faith (1st Timothy 6:12). It takes good associate pastors and team leaders to fulfill God's call on a lead pastor's life.

I highly recommend this book as a training manual for all church staff. Thank you, Pastor Lee, for this great book and for being an armorbearer to me these many years.

Duane Sheriff

Table of Contents

A few of the truths we will explore throughout this book

- Anyone who serves a leader is an Armourbearer

- Every great leader was once an Armourbearer

- Not every Armourbearer becomes a great senior leader

- Armourbearers are vital to any ministry success

- There's a process to becoming an Armourbearer

- Be faithful with what God has given others

- You are sowing to your future

Chapter 1

What is an Armourbearer?

Anyone who helps a leader is an Armourbearer!

{<><><>}

Armourbearers are not after their leader's positions or possessions. They are not just an Old Testament concept about individuals, who killed their leaders, as some have taught. As a matter of fact, scripturally just the opposite is true. One of the greatest Armourbearers, "David, the shepherd boy," had his leader "King Saul' attempt to kill him at least thirteen recorded times (without any retaliation from his armourbearer) and in I Sam. 23:14, it says "Saul sought him every day" to kill him!

No, beloved, a modern-day armourbearer loves his/her leader and their leader loves them. An Armourbearer is anyone of the thousands of unheralded servants who hold up the leader's arms in times of battle like Aaron and Hur did for Moses, (Exodus 17:12). They are the servant leaders who make ministry happen every day and in every way. Servants without whom every ministry on the planet would absolutely cease to exist. The modern-day Armourbearers are the backbone of every ministry everywhere! They are the humble warriors who fight for their Kings' honor and are willing to follow after their leader's heart (I Sam. 14:7) in an effort to see God's work and will be done!!!!

I Sam. 14:1 "Now it came to pass upon that day, that Jonathon the son of Saul said unto the young man that **bare his armour,** Come, let us go over to the Philistines' garrison, that is on the other side. But he told not his father."

The simplest explanation and definition of an Armourbearer is this: he was the man who carried the king's, or leader's armor into battle! However, the Armourbearer was so much more than just someone who carried some weapons into battle. He was one of the king's most trusted and loyal servants because the king's life was quite literally in his hands! When you're in the heat of a battle (which leaders often are) you cannot be concerned about the loyalty or commitment of the leaders you're connected to. From hereafter, I will refer to all who serve another person/leader, as "Armourbearers." If a leader is unable to trust his/her Armourbearers, they're fighting with a handicap. It would be like fighting blindfolded, on one leg, with one arm tied behind your back. So, unless you are a Ninja warrior, there's little chance of winning any real battle! If you couldn't trust your staff and co-laborers in the kingdom of God, then you would be constantly concerned about attacks from behind you. The need to look back and defend yourself from attacks from behind would render you ineffective and virtually harmless (ineffective) against the enemy in front of you. Many leaders today are doing battle with this handicap. This was the main role of an Armourbearer: to do battle against the attacks that came from behind. Not only did he carry the leader's weapons into battle, but he himself also fought the battle that was going on behind the leader. He followed the leader, courageously defending off all attacks from the rear so the leader could put his full attention on moving forward and advancing the kingdom. This man had to be trusted with the very life of the leader they followed!

In modern-day terminology, an Armourbearer would be anyone who assists a Pastor or leader. Whether you realize it or not, many ministries today have collapsed or been unfruitful because Armourbearers didn't defend their leader. They didn't go to battle against the attacks from behind. I believe that the problem with many ministries today is spiritual "staph infection." There are many interesting facts about staph infection in the natural realm that have spiritual implications and I think you'll find those facts enlightening.

- Staph infection left unattended can lead to death!
- 80% of all people carry this infection even though they themselves are not affected by it. They may not even know they're carriers of this infection, but they still infect others.

- Infected people can and do transfer their infection to others when they are exposed to the open sores and injuries of others.

- The people most likely to spread staph infection are the people who are in jobs that help people – jobs like doctors, nurses, teachers, pastors, greeters or things of that nature.

Now that's a message that will preach! My sincere desire is that I can help both the servant leader and the Armourbearer find and fulfill their God-given roles in the kingdom! This will allow us to combine our efforts and truly synergize as we fight the same enemy (and not each other).

Armourbearers are the warrior servants who help support their leaders in the battle we call ministry. Part of the problem in church culture is that most people were raised in a totem pole concept concerning ministry. This is where the senior pastor is at the top of the totem pole, and then there is the associate pastor just below him, then on and on down the totem pole until you get to the rest of us. This is just wrong because ministry is not a totem pole at all; it's a river, where everything flows from the throne of God and brings life to everything it touches. The issue has never been about your place in the kingdom but rather your obedience to God in His kingdom! If you do what God has called you to do, no matter what that is, you will hear God say, "Well done thou good and faithful servant." If, however, you become something God never intended you to be, then what did you truly accomplish?

What we need is Armourbearers who see their role as one of honor and integrity. Today's Armourbearers are not called Armourbearers but they are just as important and just as needed. These individuals include, but are not limited to, associate pastors, worship leaders, youth pastors, children's church workers, media staff, ushers, and greeters, etc. These are the servants who have captured the heart of their leader, as well as knowing what's in his heart. Too many ministries today have people who have been hired to fill a role but never became a true Armourbearer, knowing the heart of their leader. These individuals are a part of the ministry, but for nothing more than a paycheck and not for the furtherance of God's kingdom. They do not know their leader's heart, nor do they care to know! It makes all the difference in the world in any ministry if the support staff does what they are supposed to do: support! And they can't truly support until they have their leader's heart and he has their heart, as well. What I mean by having their leader's heart is: they know his vision for that ministry. They know what makes him come to life and what weighs him down. They're aware of his strengths and weaknesses - so much so that they can sense when he's tired and needs someone to hold up his arms as Aaron and Hur did for Moses. Ministry can be extremely taxing and a heavy burden to bear.

Moses came to a breaking point in his ministry. The needs and problems had become so overwhelming; he was so tired of the congregation's murmuring and complaining that he wanted God to take his life!

Numbers 11: 11-15 (Verse 11) "And Moses said unto the Lord, Wherefore hast thou afflicted thy servant? And wherefore have I not found favor in thy sight, that thou layest the burden of all this people upon me?"
(Verse 12) "Have I conceived all this people? Have I begotten them, that thou shouldest say unto me, Carry them in thy bosom, as a nursing father beareth the sucking child, unto the

land which thou swarest unto their fathers?"

(Verse 13) "Whence should I have flesh to give unto all this people? For they weep unto me, saying, Give us flesh, that we may eat!"

(Verse 14) "I am not able to bear all this people alone, because it is too heavy for me."

(Verse 15) "And if thou deal thus with me, kill me, I pray thee, out of hand, if I have found favor in thy sight; and let me not see my wretchedness."

If you've been pastoring or leading for more than six months, you understand his situation and his cry to the Lord. Maybe you've cried this to the Lord, as well? Pastor Moses was at his wit's end and he's telling God: these are not my children to take care of. If this is the way that ministry is going to, be just kill me, take me out, it's more than I can bear alone (and it will be more than you and I can bear alone, as well)! God's answer to this situation is very relevant to all of us in ministry today. So, what is God's answer? Glad you asked. His answer was Armourbearers! He didn't call them that; he called them Elders with the same spirit as their leader, which is by its very description an Armourbearer!

Let's read from Numbers, chapter 11 (Verse 16) "And the Lord said unto Moses, Gather unto me seventy men of the elders of Israel, whom thou knowest to be the elders of the people, and officers over them; and bring them unto the tabernacle of the congregation, that they may stand there with thee."

(Verse 17) "And I will come down and talk with thee there: and I will take the spirit which is upon thee, and will put it upon them;

and they shall bear the burden of the people with thee, that thou bear it not thyself alone."

10 Powerful Truths from These Scriptures

1) Ministry is too hard for anyone to do alone!
    > "...because it's too heavy for me."

2) God has the answer.
    > " … and the Lord said unto Moses..."

3) Elders are Armourbearers with the same spirit as their leaders.
    > "…. I will take the spirit which is upon thee, and I will put it upon them…"

4) Elders already showed signs of being a good leader.
    > "...whom thou knowest to be elders..."

5) These people are brought to Moses through the church.
    > "… and bring them into the tabernacle..."

6) Elders/Armourbearers stand with their leader.
    > " ... that they may stand there with thee..."

7) God has to speak to the leader about this.
    > "...and I will talk with thee there..."

8) God has to put the spirit of the leaders upon the
    Armourbearers!
    >   "...and I will put it upon them..."

9) Armourbearers are people who help carry the burden of the
    people with you.
    >   "...and they shall bear the burden of the people with
    >   thee..."

10)   The leader will always have a burden for the people.
    >   "...shall bear the burden of the people with thee...

Moses was aware of the benefits of having true Armourbearers
in his time of need. We will look at a few short but powerful
verses and then extract some of the truths from those
scriptures.

Exodus 17:8-13 (Verse 8) "Then came Amalek and fought with
Israel in Rephidim."
(Verse 9) "And Moses said unto Joshua, Choose us out men,
and go out, fight with Amalek: tomorrow I will stand on the top of
the hill with the rod of God in mine hand."
(Verse 10) "So Joshua did as Moses had said to him, and fought
with Amalek: and Moses, Aaron, and Hur went up to the top of
the hill."
(Verse 11) "And it came to pass, when Moses held up his hand,
that Israel prevailed: and when he let down his hand, Amalek
prevailed."

(Verse 12) "But Moses' hands were heavy; and they took a stone, and put it under him, and he sat thereon; and Aaron and Hur stayed up his hands, the one on the one side, and the other on the other side; and his hands were steady until the going down of the sun." (Verse 13) "And Joshua discomfited Amalek and his people with the edge of the sword." Armourbearers do what they've been asked. That's one of the greatest miracles and changes needed today; people doing what they are told: " … and Joshua did as Moses said."

Moses led the battle by being where the people could see him and be encouraged by it: " …. and I will stand on the top of the hill."

Armourbearers understand that the emotional, physical and spiritual state of their leaders affect them: "And it came to pass, when Moses held up his hand, that Israel prevailed: and when he let down his hand, Amalek prevailed."

When the leader's hands are up (representing strength & worship) the whole church finds victory: "Israel prevailed."

Ministry is too heavy to be carried alone: "…but Moses' hands were heavy."

Armourbearers see the need and meet the need without having to be told: "And they took a stone, and put it under him, and he sat thereon; and Aaron and Hur stayed up his hands."

Armourbearers allow their leaders to rest (on the rock/ Jesus

Christ): " …and he sat thereon."

They hold up the leader's hands (representing ministry) until the battle has been won: "… and his hands were steady until the going down of the sun."

Chapter 2

What Armourbearers Do

{<><><>}

The modern-day Armourbearer's list of assignments, functions, and duties are virtually without end. They sweep the spectrum of everything from helping in the children's church to picking up senior citizens for a Sunday service. Anything from the obvious parking lot attendant to those in the unseen media ministries. They teach youth groups, Sunday school classes, and Bible studies; and they also defend their leaders against those who murmur, complain and bring accusations against the ministry and the leadership. The modern-day Armourbearer is called by a multitude of names in today's culture. Here are a few you might recognize: servant/leader, a minister of helps, those in support ministry, a volunteer, an assistant, associate, or minister, secretary, usher or custodian. In the Kingdom of God, none of these is more important than the other. They just differ in their function and responsibility. Like an eye or a hand, both must do their part if your body is to function properly!

I Sam. 14:7 "And his Armourbearer said unto him, do all that is in thy heart: turn thee; behold, I am with thee according to thy heart."

The main thing an Armourbearer does is serve; in whatever is in the heart of their leader for them to do! The Armourbearer is not for you to use like a "get out of jail" or "free pass" so that you use them for whatever you don't like to do, or decisions that may create controversy. That's not an Armourbearer. That would be a pallbearer and it will be your funeral! Please notice the word "behold" in this verse, "behold, I am with thee." It's a very important word because it means to see, observe, to be held by; literally lo, also (as experiencing surprise). Now, do you remember what Jesus said in Matt. 28:20, "And, lo, I am with you always, even unto the end of the world."? Well, it's the same word used in the Old Testament. "Behold." Jesus was saying, "look, observe, see as if you're surprised. I'm here with thee also!" That is what Jonathon's Armourbearer was saying to his leader: Behold (look, observe, see), I'm here, also. Most of the leaders I know wouldn't have to act as if they were experiencing surprise at seeing their staff standing with them in battle. They would be genuinely surprised. It is going to take a new kind of thinking in our ministries for us to see real Armourbearers raised up; servant warriors who can be counted on when their ministries are in the heat of the battle to be there, also!

Three Awesome Armourbearers

II Sam 23:8-17 (Verse 8) "These be the names of the mighty men whom David had: The Tachmonite that sat in the seat, chief among the captains; the same was Adino the Eznite: he lift

up his spear against eight hundred, whom he slew at one time."
(Verse 9) "And after him was Eleazar the son of Dodo the Ahohite,
one of the three mighty men with David, when they defied the
Philistines that were there gathered together to battle, and the
men of Israel were gone away."

(Verse 10) "He arose, and smote the Philistines until his hand was
weary, and his hand clave unto the sword: and the LORD wrought
a great victory that day; and the people returned after him only to
spoil."

(Verse 11) "And after him was Shammah the son of Agee the
Hararite. And the Philistines were gathered together into a
troop, where was a piece of ground full of lentiles: and the
people fled from the Philistines."

(Verse 12) "But he stood in the midst of the ground, and
defended it, and slew the Philistines: and the LORD wrought a
great victory."

(Verse 13) "And three of the thirty chief went down, and came
to David in the harvest time unto the cave of Adullam: and the
troop of the Philistines pitched in the valley of Rephaim." (Verse
14) "And David was then in an hold, and the garrison of the
Philistines was then in Bethlehem."

(Verse 15) "And David longed, and said, Oh that one would give
me drink of the water of the well of Bethlehem, which is by the
gate!"

(Verse 16) "And the three mighty men brake through the host of
the Philistines, and drew water out of the well of Bethlehem, that
was by the gate, and took it, and brought it to David: nevertheless
he would not drink thereof, but poured it out unto the LORD."

(Verse 17) "And he said, Be it far from me, O LORD, that I

should do this: is not this the blood of the men that went in jeopardy of their lives? Therefore he would not drink it. These things did these three mighty men."

Those are some real God-anointed, God-appointed, devil-stomping Armourbearers! Now, be honest. Wouldn't you love to have that kind of commitment and loyalty from your team members; individuals who would break through an enemy's army, get a glass of water (the type and kind you asked for), and then break back through that same army just to bring you that glass of water? Wouldn't you love to have people with that kind of heart and desire to defend you? Well, you can, and you do; they're just disguised as people with problems! To fully understand how David accomplished this kind of covenant relationship with his warrior servants (AKA: Armourbearers), one must see where these mighty men came from. The revelation of where these men originated from will be both encouraging and very challenging at the same time. Let's read it together.

I Sam 22:1-2 (Verse 1) "David therefore departed thence and escaped to the cave Adullam: and when his brethren and all his father's house heard it, they went down thither to him."
(Verse 2) "And every one that was in distress, and everyone that was in debt, and everyone that was discontented, gathered themselves unto him; and he became a captain over them: and there were with him about four hundred men."

Here is the revelation many leaders need to embrace:

Armourbearers like the ones mentioned above start out as sheep that are really messed up and in need, just like your sheep! This kind of loyalty and commitment doesn't come cheap or by wishing for it. You must get it the old fashioned way, the Old Testament way, you must earn it the same way David did; by sowing commitment and loyalty into the lives of others when they were not so strong and not so mighty. When I read the description of those who joined David in the cave of Adullam, it sounds like the description of most of our congregations. Everyone who was in debt (they're of little or no help financially), in distress (they're of little or no help emotionally), and discontented (they're seldom, if ever, satisfied) joined themselves unto him. Have you ever heard the phrase, "Birds of a feather flock together"? Well, this is a fitting phrase for why these men joined David. At this point in his life, he was a man on the run and in trouble with the law. These future Armourbearers would have felt right at home in his company. This is where David's three mighty men were introduced to him. Notice what followed the description of these would-be covenantal members: "And he became a captain over them."

He became a captain over them, meaning they chose to let him lead. Never forget if you oversee anything or anyone today, it is because others have chosen to let you! David earned loyalty and commitment from these mighty men by being loyal and committed to them in their times of need. Let me explain. Have you ever walked someone through a traumatic experience? Ever helped someone get through an addiction, the loss of a loved one, a debilitating bout with depression? It's exhausting work; there's lots of encouragement and energy going out with very little, if any, return (at least at first). It takes a real commitment and loyalty to people to accomplish any lasting change in situations like that. I know. I've been blessed enough to help many people through those exact situations and lived long enough to see real, lasting change. The most amazing by-product of those encounters, to me, is the love and commitment these people have for me. Many of them have stated and proven they would lay down their life for me! On a more personal note, that is to a large degree why I'm so committed to my role as Armourbearer to Pastor Duane. My family and I have gone through some extremely painful situations and Pastor Duane and his family were right there committed to seeing us through those situations. They stuck by our side when others would have dropped us like a bad habit. So if you, as a leader, are going to see real God-anointed, God-appointed, devil-stomping Armourbearers in your church, you must be faithful to love those nobody wants and then God will give you people everybody wants.

So be sure and "love the ones you're with" (sounds like a song). If you sow to this, you will

reap in due time by creating loyalty and commitment that will come back to you in waves!!!

Chapter 3

The Seven Tests Every Armourbearer Must Face

{<><><>}

There is a truth many people try to avoid. That truth is: God tests the hearts of men and women! Deut. 8:2 is a perfect example of this. Let me paraphrase what God tells His people. Remember why we have wilderness experiences: to humble us, to prove (meaning to test) us, to know what's in our hearts and to see if we will keep His commandments. These tests are almost always a surprise test. This is the best way for us and for God to know what's in our hearts. The tests in life are unavoidable. We can't cheat or manipulate the results because it's God who's grading the test and the results! The good news is that God has already given you the answer in Deut. 30:19, "Choose life!"

#1) Test of Heart: I Sam. 16:7

"But the Lord said unto Samuel, look not on his countenance, or on the height of his stature; because I have refused him: for the Lord seeth not as man seeth; for man looketh on the outward appearance, but the Lord looketh on the heart."

There is nothing more important to you and your life than what's in your heart! What's in your heart affects every other area of your life. The scriptures reveal this truth in so many ways. For the sake of time, we will only look at a few. Prov. 4:23 says "Keep thy heart with all diligence; for out of it are the issues of life."

The way I often share this scripture is to "Guard your heart like a prison guard, watching what comes in and what goes out of a prison. Because out of your heart flow the issues of life. One of the definitions of the word issues is "boundaries." So, out of your heart come your "set boundaries" in life. If you have attitudes of feeling small, insignificant, unwanted and unloved, those feelings originate from the set boundaries in your heart. If the things you say about yourself sound something like "No one likes me, no one would even miss me if I just disappeared, I have nothing to offer anyone, and I'm a mistake just waiting to happen..." those thoughts come from your heart. They are boundaries in your heart that keep you locked into a mindset that limits where you will go and what you will do in this life. In Matt. 12:34, the Bible once again shows how important your heart is, "For out of the abundance of the heart the mouth speaks." So what you say about yourself comes from your heart – and if you say it long enough, it will become what you believe. And if you believe it long enough, your actions will line up perfectly with what's in your heart! Simply stated: the actions you perform originate from the thoughts of your heart. Therefore, what you let in and out of your heart is vitally important.

Notice this again in Prov. 4:20-22 (Verse 20) "My son, attend to my words; incline thine ear unto my sayings."
(Verse 21) "Let them not depart from thine eyes; keep them in the midst of thine heart."
(Verse 22} "For they are life unto those that find them, and health to all their flesh."

If we place God's Words in our hearts, the result is life and health. I'd say that's kind of important. So, if we're sick in our body or our minds, we can bring health to those areas by putting God's Word in our hearts, in abundance, so that out of your mouth will come blessings and therefore life.

The heart test can only be passed by us intentionally filling our hearts with God's Word. Deut. 30:19 states emphatically, "I call heaven and earth to record this day against you, that I have set before you life and death, blessing and cursing: therefore choose life, that both thou and thy seed may live." Life is a choice, not a chance! We can choose what goes in and we can choose what comes out of our hearts – it's our choice! The Lord showed me a long time ago that what comes into my heart and what comes out of my heart is like what I allow to come in or out of my house. I'm responsible to let things in and out of my home that is good and positive and beneficial. I'm also responsible to not let things in or out that can hurt or harm myself or others.

You can fool me; you can fool others but what you can't do is fool God! He looks at your heart. You and the condition of your heart are vitally important to your future. Keeping your heart right is the key to all things that are good and things that are of God. He knows if you're doing something to be seen of men, or because you truly want to serve. He knows if you're truly humble or just trying to act humble! We must trust that God knows our hearts and what is best for us. Then and only then can we rest in God promoting us in this life or us remaining where we are. We are to be like a tree planted, that bears fruit "in its time."

One more item of interest concerning the seven tests we all must take in leadership: the tests will generally be a pop quiz! Like almost all of the tests of the kingdom, you won't know it's coming until the test is being given, and the teacher isn't likely going to talk to you much "except for a few words of affirmation" until the test is over! So keep guarding your heart and you will keep passing the test!

#2) The Test of Insignificance: I Sam. 16:1-11

I Sam. 16:11(MSG Bible) "Then he asked Jesse, "Is this it? Are there no more sons?" "Well yes, there's the runt. But he's out tending the sheep."

Have you ever been the last one picked for a team, or not picked at all? David was treated even worse than that. David wasn't even given the opportunity to not be picked!

The test of feeling insignificant is a test we will all face and we must all pass. Being overlooked by leadership is a common occurrence that the enemy uses to create offense in our hearts. More people miss their destiny because of being offended more than almost any other problem. David was certainly tested in the area of insignificance and passed with flying colors!

The prophet Samuel is commanded by God to anoint the next King of Israel (I Sam. 16:1). That man is to come from the household of Jesse. Now you need to understand the gravity of this visit from the prophet. Samuel is one of the godliest men on the planet and he's coming to your house, to anoint someone from your household "you or one of your siblings" to be the next King of Israel. In other words, one of you is to become one of the most powerful men on the planet, AND, YOUR FATHER DIDN'T EVEN INVITE YOU TO THE MEETING! You are not even given the opportunity to not be picked. Your father considered you such an unlikely candidate, he didn't even bother to invite you to the meeting! That kind of rejection most of us have faced before. Unfortunately, it is entirely possible, if not probable, that we will face it numerous times in our walk of faith. Anyone seeking to be used by God will take this test, including God's Son. Remember the temptation of Jesus in the wilderness, "if you are the Son of God, command these stones to become bread?" It was a test of his identity and his significance.

For us to pass the test of insignificance we must learn that it can never be accomplished through acquiring titles, an office, or being invited to the right meetings. Instead, we find that true significance is found in doing and being what you were created to do and be. Jesus said it best in John 17:4, "I have glorified thee on earth: I have finished the work thou gavest me to do." Then in Matt. 17:5, Jesus hears his Father God say "...this is my Beloved Son, in whom I'm well pleased." Talk about feeling significant! I don't think I can overemphasize this truth. The true source of significance is knowing God is well pleased with you. I encourage you to seek the honor that comes from God and not from man. If you have the honor of God, you will in time have the honor of man. Seek to hear your Heavenly Father say daily, "Well done, thou good and faithful servant" and in doing so, you will always feel significant!

#3) The Test of Being Whole: "Spirit, Soul, and Body":
I Sam. 16:12

I Sam. 16:12 (MSG Bible), "Jesse sent for him. He was brought in, the very picture of health bright eyed, good looking."

Taking care of ourselves is the best thing we can do for those who depend on us. If we don't take care of ourselves, why would we think other people would want or trust us to take care of them?

I agree that one bad apple doesn't spoil the whole bunch, but I also believe that one bad apple can make all the other apples look bad! Being the "picture of health" goes considerably deeper than just eating bagels and doing karate class once a week. David was healthy in all three areas of his life, "spirit, soul, and body." I think we should take care of ourselves and our physical body as a part of that equation. As my Pastor says, "I know the Bible says that bodily exercise profiteth little but, you needeth the littleth it profiteth." I agree! I run three miles every day except Sunday; not to compete or to brag but because I want to be ministering when I'm in my 90's. Being healthy in our body doesn't mean we should all have ripped abs and muscles that rival Arnold Schwarzenegger or that we must wear suits and ties. It just means we can't neglect the temple of God. If we can't control our flesh in simple acts of obedience to things like fasting, tithing, running or just not eating that fourth donut, we probably won't be able to discipline other areas of our life either. We must be faithful in the little things so we can be faithful in greater things.

I believe we should bathe, brush our teeth and wear decent clothes. Our leaders shouldn't have to make excuses for our appearance! However, having said that, I believe that true health starts with our spirit man and works its way out to our physical man. Godly people are attractive because of what's on the inside of them: "Christ in you, the hope of glory." When we have a genuine relationship with God, it shows in how we look and what we do! The lost people of Jesus' time were attracted to him. Sinners liked hanging out with Him. Why? His relationship with God was so obvious in His actions and attitudes that it caused Him to be someone others truly liked being with. This is how every Christian's life should be and it should be true of all Armourbearers.

We should be healthy in our soul, as well as in our mind, will, and emotions. Our soul is the most difficult part of our triune being to stay healthy in. Our body is what we call "amoral." That means it's neither good nor bad, it's just a container. It's our earth suit. Like a drinking glass, it is neither good nor bad. It just depends on what you put in it. If that glass is filled with water, it brings life; if it's filled with cyanide poison, it will bring death. So, while our body matters, it's our soul that causes us the most trouble. It must be renewed daily (Eph. 4:23). For instance, if you're thinking about something sad and depressing (like the loss of a job), your emotions will line up by being sad, depressed and possibly angry. This will result in your actions having a lack of energy, tears, and/or maybe even violent behavior. The opposite is also true – if you're thinking about something good, a new baby in the family, or other blessings, then your emotions will likely be that of joy, excitement, and delight which will, in turn, result in active, energetic, tireless deeds and labors of love. The problem is that in all of these areas of our soul we are so easily affected. The simplest of things can cause major problems. If we lose a piece of paper (that's called money), we feel bad. If we find that same piece of paper, we feel great joy. If someone makes a positive comment about our hair, we feel good about ourselves – but if someone asks what happened to our hair, we can become almost instantly depressed over it. I've often stated that as a people we're only happy about three days out of the year. We're always complaining about something it seems, "it's too hot, it's too cold, it's raining, it's not raining, it's Monday." We must constantly be renewed in our minds to biblical truths like "This is the day the Lord has made, I will rejoice and be glad in it" and "Do all things without murmurings and disputings." We need to think on the right things and make sure our actions reflect our heart and our Christian values. This is what the Apostle Paul was communicating in 2 Cor. 10:3-6 where he makes it abundantly clear that the battle is our mind. Take a good look at these verses with me and specifically the words I've underlined.

2 Cor. 10:3 -6 (Verse 3) "For though we walk in the flesh, we do not war after the flesh:
(Verse 4) "For the weapons of our warfare are not carnal, but mighty through God to the pulling down of strongholds"
(Verse 5) "Casting down imaginations, and every high thing that exalteth itself against the knowledge of God, and bringing into captivity every tthought to the obedience of Christ."
(Verse 6) "And having in a readiness to revenge all disobedience, when your obedience is fulfilled."

Notice how the weapons we use are directly connected to our thoughts. We are to pull down strongholds. Strongholds are places in our minds where the enemy feels safe. We're to cast down imaginations and anything that exalts itself against our knowledge of God. Our imaginations are pictures that are created in our minds. There are literally thousands of things the enemy uses against our knowledge of God. We know in our mind that God is good, but a thought comes and says, "If God is good why did you lose your job?" We have the knowledge that God is for us and not against us but then there's the thought, "If God is for me then why is there so much hardship in my life?" Finally, Paul says we're to take captive "like a prisoner" every thought! In our minds is where the battle must be won. If you've ever tried to take your thoughts captive and agree with what God says you should be thinking on, you know exactly what I mean. You determine in your heart to stay positive at work all day long no matter what happens, and before you leave your driveway you're upset! I absolutely love the Word of God, the Bible. I love the way it not only tells us what we should do; it also tells us why we should do it. In Philippians 4:8, Paul shares some things we should be thinking on: The things that are true, honest, just, pure and lovely, of a good report, the things that are virtuous, and praiseworthy. That's an awesome list, and he goes on to explain why we should think about these things. He says that the benefits of keeping our minds focused on these things are "The God of peace will be with us!" When we focus and think on God's Word, we have peace. Inward peace leads to outward health. Our soul being healthy is the by-product of walking in the truth. It's also God's desire for us. In III John, the Apostle John shows us this truth.

III John 1:2-4 (Verse 2) "Beloved, I wish above all things that thou mayest prosper and be in health, even as thy soul prospereth."

(Verse 3) "For I rejoiced greatly, when the brethren came and testified of the truth that is in thee, even as thou walkest in the truth."

(Verse 4) "I have no greater joy than to hear that my children walk in truth."

John says his greatest desire and joy in life is hearing that those people he'd influenced to follow the Lord (he called them his children) walked in truth. The health of our soul is directly connected to the truth we're walking out in our daily lives. Always remember that your mind, will, and emotions will never be more prosperous or healthy than the amount of God's Word you read and understand.

You are a spiritual being, you have a soul and you live in a body. Because you are a spiritual being, you're going to live eternally somewhere. The good news is that you get to choose where that eternal dwelling place is. That's what hell is: an eternal dwelling place. An eternal jail for those spiritual people who rejected God's goodness, His grace and His free offer of salvation. When your spirit (little "s") accepts Christ's offer of salvation through the Holy Spirit (big "S"), you are born again and you become a resident of God's kingdom. You are a new creature entirely, from the inside out. You look the same as before, but your life is now hid with God in Christ (Col. 3:3). You're an entirely new creature. God will begin to change you from the inside out into something that reflects the very image of Christ to the world. This understanding that you're a "triune being" (spirit, soul, and body) can change your outlook on life. It answers so many questions about why we can still sin after being born again; why we can forgive and still have feelings that contradict that choice, and things of that nature.

#4) The Test of Significance: I Sam. 16:13

I Sam 16:13, "Then Samuel took the horn of oil, and anointed him in the midst of his brethren: and the Spirit of the Lord came upon David from that day forward."

So, Samuel rose up and went to Ramah. Again, we must realize the importance and magnitude of this event: being anointed by Samuel as the next king! Only then can we fully appreciate the pressure and the warfare David came under. If David was like the average person, he would have immediately changed his "walk" to a "strut." He would have pranced around, acting high and mighty, demanding others treat him with respect, commanding others to do his bidding and expecting they fulfill his every wish. Instead, David goes right back to tending sheep and being ridiculed by his older brothers (I Sam 17:28).

In contrast, King Saul didn't pass the test of being recognized. I don't know if you've read the account of Saul's induction into being King of Israel. But Saul was God's choice! God said in I

Sam. 9:17, "And when Samuel saw Saul, the LORD said unto him, Behold the man whom I spake to thee of! This same shall reign over my people." At this time in Saul's life, he was the right man. He was humble and he loved the Lord. Something terrible happened between the time he was anointed King and the time when he sought to kill another human being (David) every day (I Sam. 23:14)!!! Look it up. From I Samuel, chapter 18 to I Samuel, chapter 27, Saul attempts to kill David a recorded thirteen times. Even worse, in I Sam. 23:14, it says he sought to do so every day!

So, what happened? Inquiring minds want to know! I believe the answer is found in I Sam. 18:7-9 (Verse 7) "And the women answered one another as they played, and said, Saul hath slain his thousands, and David his ten thousands."
(Verse 8) "And Saul was very wroth, and the saying displeased him; and he said, They have ascribed unto David ten thousands, and to me they have ascribed but thousands: and what can he have more but the kingdom?"
(Verse 9) "And Saul eyed David from that day and forward."

Two problems jump to the forefront of my mind when I read this.
#1) Recognition of someone else's strength revealed the pride in Saul's heart. He couldn't stand that David was being honored above him. Instead of seeing David's strength as a warrior was to his benefit, he became angry and then bitterness set in until his whole life's ambition was to kill David. He saw David as competition and not as an ally. He had to be

seen as the best "at everything." This is the test we will all have to take. It's hard not being chosen, but it's even harder being chosen and not changing; not letting it go to your head. Many times, I've seen this happen. A volunteer is doing an incredible job at something. They bring excellence to a task and others love working with them. They're a joy to be around and they reflect Christ in them. Then they are hired to do that job and almost overnight they change, like a Dr. Jekyll and Mr. Hyde kind of change. They become bossy and demanding. They feel they should be treated differently than their volunteers. It's a very painful thing to observe and to be involved in and seldom do they receive loving correction about it.

#2) He feared losing his position. His exact words were, "What more can he have but the kingdom?" This is another area that we must guard our hearts against. Remember, there's always someone more gifted, talented, smarter, and better equipped than you. If you love the ministry, you're a part of more than your own selfish ambition and title – you will want the best person doing the job. I've personally replaced myself many times with people more capable and better suited than I was for a particular job or task. It's always benefitted the team and because the team sees my willingness to do what's right for the team and not just me, they let me lead. Yes, I said, "they let me lead." You may think you're in charge because you're so much better than your co-workers. The irrefutable truth is if you're leading, it's because they let you. Unless you're a dictator, they do have the choice to leave for any reason they deem proper and they will; even if you are smarter, stronger, more capable or whatever; if you're mean, selfish, self-centered, condescending or a hundred other bad flaws in your character that can be mentioned, trust me – they will leave.

Saul should have "and could have" been the benefactor of one of history's greatest warriors being his personal bodyguard! He could have slept with great peace knowing David was his protector. Instead, his pride and insecurities blinded him to these truths "and they'll blind us too" if we don't guard our hearts. We should never be intimidated by the strengths of those God has placed in our life. On the contrary, we should be humbled and excited that God would send them to us and that they would choose to hear God and use those strengths to help do something great in the Kingdom of God. Promotion comes from God and God alone. So, there's no real place for pride or arrogance. It's all God and that makes it all good.

#5) The Test of Becoming: I Sam 16:21

I Sam 16:21, "And David came to Saul, and stood before him: and he loved him greatly; and he became his Armourbearer."

There's a process every time to becoming an active positive part of any ministry. Many anointed ministers never reach their full potential because they don't want to earn their stripes, put in their time, and show themselves faithful. I have two analogies I use to help people understand why there's a process and why it's necessary. Let me share those two examples with you now.

#1) Everyone's a can with no label: If you go to a grocery store and buy a discounted can because the label is missing, you can shake the can and guess what's in it: corn, fruit cocktail, hominy or something worse (if there is such a thing), or you can call the can whatever you have need of at the time. I need a can of corn so I'll call this can: corn. But the best way to see what's in the can is to simply take the time to open it up and see what's inside. Then you can accurately say what's in the can. People are a lot like that can with no label. Most of the time they can't tell me what they are, or I could shake them (not recommended) and then guess what they are, or I could call them whatever I have need of at the time: Youth Pastor, Children's Church Pastor, Worship Leader. Or I could simply spend the time to see what's in them. Most ministries are in such desperate need of help that they find the can, the person with no label and call it whatever they're in need of at the time! This, more often than not, leads to everyone involved being hurt, confused and disillusioned about ministry! Take the time to see what's inside them and then call them what they are, by the grace of God.

#2) No one should buy their stripes. If you've ever seen anyone in the military or watched a Veteran's Day Parade, you'll see the stripes on their uniform, along with their respective badges and pins. Those emblems all represent some deed or accomplishment. They were earned with blood, sweat, and tears. No one gave them anything and they certainly didn't buy them! They received those stripes the hard way – they earned them! It took time, commitment, and endless hours of training, exercise, and sacrifice. When someone goes down to the army surplus store and buys their stripes, they unintentionally make a mockery of all those who earned their stripes. They bypassed any of the hard work. They didn't have to prove themselves capable. They didn't do one sit-up or run one mile carrying a weapon and heavy backpack. They didn't earn their stripes by becoming a trained, battle-ready soldier. They bought their stripes. That's not bad enough. These would-be soldiers, these imposters, if called upon to fulfill the role that those stripes represent, they would fail miserably and possibly put other innocent people's lives in jeopardy because of it.

It's possible right now to go online and buy a minister's license for about $35.00 off the internet. With very little (if any) training or commitment other than your $35.00. The problem is you "bought your stripes!" You didn't earn them through endless hours of prayer and Bible study. You didn't wrestle with the call of God on your life and His will to be a minister. You weren't in the trenches day after day wrestling with helping others through loss and pain. You didn't wade through the scriptures day after day believing for the wisdom of God to help you meet the needs of the people God entrusted to you. You didn't struggle with learning to hear God's voice or recognizing the Holy Spirit's prompting. You didn't suffer the ridicule and persecution that comes from following the Lord. You bought your stripes for $35.00!

Here's a question you need to answer: Do you want to work

with someone who's taken the time to get to know you, your ministry and your ministry's culture, someone who's proven they can be trusted, someone who you know, someone who works well with the team, someone who's been in the trenches with you and smells like sheep? Or would you want a hireling; someone who bought their credentials for $35.00, someone whose only sacrifice into ministry was a $35.00 investment? This is why we must yield to the process of becoming an Armourbearer.

This is a *very* real process – one that I have chosen to call "the process of becoming'.' Let's take a closer look at this process as it is revealed through the life of David. In I Sam. 16:21, we see in part that process of David becoming the king's Armourbearer. Notice: "And David came to Saul, and stood before him; and loved him greatly, and he became his Armourbearer."

Three major keys mentioned in this process:
#1) He stood before him
#2) He loved him greatly
#3) He became his Armourbearer

#1) He stood before him:
For many years I *oversaw* the maintenance and special projects at the church I served in. It involved painting whole sections of the church, building new handrails or walkways, removing lights or damaged equipment and then overseeing

their replacement and cleanup of the entire grounds, just to mention just a few items. So, I spent my whole day working with as many as 100+ volunteers. There was one thing that was consistent from year to year no matter what or how many projects we had. I was never able to use anyone that didn't show up! Many people truly want to be used by God and be involved in ministry but, if they're not available, "they just can't and won't be used." Every leader I know is forced to use those who show up and those who show up are not always the most talented. That's real life in the ministry. I believe we should always do our best to get the *very* best we can and desire things to be done in excellence but, we are all forced to use those who show up. Jesus used those who heeded the call and showed up. If Jesus had to use those who showed up, we will have to use those who show up!

Every leader I know on a scale of 1-10 wants people who are 10s at everything they're given to do every time. However, as a general rule, we don't get people who are at a level 10 as a leader. We very often get people who are a 5 (sometimes less) and we must develop them into 10s. A little side note: I agree with John Maxwell's "Law of the Lid" in which he so eloquently shares: If you're a 7 in your leadership skills (on a scale of 1-10), then you can only raise people to a level 6 in their leadership skills. If you want them to grow to a level 7, you must grow to a level 8. You must, therefore, spend enough time with them to know their level of leadership and then spend more time helping them grow to the next level. This means they must stand before you long enough to become whatever that next level is!

#2) He loved him greatly:

This is such a powerful truth that I hope I can convey clearly! If you don't love your Pastor greatly and he doesn't love you greatly, then start right now and pursue, persevere until you do. Spend time with them; learn to love them with a covenantal love, a love that is more than a feeling. Feelings are way too fickle to trust. The simplest of things affect them: rain, no rain, it's Monday. A simple compliment makes you feel great, "I really like your hair." A simple question like, "What happened to your hair?" can put you in a bad mood.

The word "love" is used so flippantly in today's world that we have no idea of the depth of what love is. We love our truck, our gun, and our dog, but we sell the truck, trade the gun and shoot the dog. So when we tell someone we love them, it's no wonder they question what we mean! When we love someone greatly, it means we're willing to lay down our lives for them. It's the kind of love a husband has for his wife, a soldier has for his comrades in arms and an Armourbearer has for his leader.

You cannot rush into this kind of commitment. To trust someone else with your very life takes time and time-tested experiences. It takes seeing faithfulness in the little things and commitment to finishing a task with excellence, even when it appears no one's looking. I'm reminded that the famous painter, Michelangelo, was once asked why he was taking so much time and care on a particular scene he was painting in the ceiling of the Sistine Chapel; a particular scene that virtually no one would ever see. His response was, "God will see." When we love someone greatly it will invoke that kind of commitment and care. I'm not asking you to "drink the Kool-Aid." I'm asking you to love your leader, to know his heart and to know he/she loves you back.

#3) He became his Armourbearer:

We are all in the process of becoming. You have spent your whole life becoming what you were destined to be the instant you were conceived. It was at that very moment your D.N.A. determined you would be male or female, short or tall, black or white. You didn't choose that; you became that! It was written in your D.N.A code and you became that person.

The Bible has many stories of people and things becoming. Here's just a few:

- Genesis 18:18 "Abraham became a great and mighty nation."
- Genesis 39:4 "Joseph became his attendant."
- Exodus 4:3 "Moses' staff became a serpent."

David went through the process of becoming at least twice. When King Saul tried to kill him, David fled to the cave of Adullam. The scriptures teach all who were in distress, in debt and discontent joined themselves unto him. And he "became a captain over them." Now you don't just declare to that group of people, "Okay, I'm your leader now." Always remember, if you're the leader of anything, it's because other people let you become their leader! This is even truer when becoming a king's/leader's Armourbearer. You literally had the King's life in your hand. He had to trust you with his very life. You didn't just announce yourself to the King as his new Armourbearer. You became it by showing yourself faithful repeatedly until the King was assured of your intentions. He knew you as a mighty warrior. As an Armourbearer, you protected the King's back. He was convinced you'd lay down your life for him, if necessary. The position was one of supreme honor and, once again, you don't demand a position like that; you become it! This is true of today's modern-day Armourbearers. You have that leader's reputation, honor and very life in your hand. If that leader has brought you into their ministry, they have demonstrated they trust you. It's up to you to become a modern-day Armourbearer.

Just as you were born a boy or a girl, you still needed to be instructed and taught how to be a boy or a girl. Do you remember, "girls don't sit like that" or "boys don't play with dolls; now pick up your GI Joe and get inside. It's time for supper"? In the same way, you must be taught, instructed how to become an Armourbearer. Every king and every leader has a certain way they desire things to be done and the Armourbearer's job is to learn those ways and desires.

We must become a worship leader, children's church pastor,

administrator or any one of the thousand other titles used for a modern-day Armourbearer. If we are called to these positions, then it is us "becoming" what we already are!

#6) The Test of Bearing Fruit: I Sam. 16:23

"And it came to pass, when the evil spirit from God was upon Saul, that David took an harp, and played with his hand: so Saul was refreshed, and was well, and the evil spirit departed from him." David could do what he was hired to do. He supplied the need he was brought in to fulfill. If you are ultimately invited to be a part of a ministry to fulfill a particular role, they are looking for you to bear fruit in that position. This may sound a little simplistic, but it's important that you do what you've been hired to do! David was sought after because the leader (King Saul) needed someone who could play skillfully and bring some relief to his tormented soul. It wasn't all that David was asked to do but it was the main thing. It led to other opportunities and eventually to the biggest advancement of his time, becoming the King of a Kingdom! It all was made possible because David did what he was brought in to do.

The Lord takes bearing fruit and not bearing fruit seriously!

John 15:1-8 (Verse 1) "I am the true vine, and my Father is the husbandman."
(Verse 2) "Every branch in me that beareth not fruit he taketh away: and every branch that beareth fruit, he purgeth it, that it may bring forth more fruit."

(Verse 3) "Now ye are clean through the word which I have spoken unto you."

(Verse 4) "Abide in me, and I in you. As the branch cannot bear fruit of itself, except it abide in the vine; no more can ye, except ye abide in me."

(Verse 5) "I am the vine, ye are the branches: He that abideth in me, and I in him, the same bringeth forth much fruit: for without me ye can do nothing."

(Verse 6) "If a man abide not in me, he is cast forth as a branch, and is withered; and men gather them, and cast them into the fire, and they are burned."

(Verse 7) "If ye abide in me, and my words abide in you, ye shall ask what ye will, and it shall be done unto you."

(Verse 8) "Herein is my Father glorified, that ye bear much fruit; so shall ye be my disciples."

"For the tree is known by his fruit." Matt. 12:33

You will never see an apple tree bear anything but an apple; or an orange tree bear anything but an orange. Everything produces after its own kind (think Genesis, chapter 1). That's one of the main reasons why we must keep our hearts right. If we have strife, bitterness or envy in our hearts, we will bear fruit that has the same DNA as us and so our fruit will be filled with strife, bitterness, and envy. We are the fruit bearers, NOT the fruit producers! The life of the tree flows from the tree out into the branches and all the branches can do is let that life flow through them. The fruit the branches bear is a by-product of abiding in, staying attached to, the tree. The branch has no life in or of itself. If you separate the branch from the tree it will wither and die. It may look alive for a little bit of time, but in reality, it was dying from the very moment it was separated from the tree. This is the truth of every Christian's life. We do not have any ability to bear fruit in and of ourselves, except we stay attached to Jesus, our life source! The instant we separate ourselves from Christ, we begin dying. We can look alive for a very small amount of time, but we are lifeless without Christ in us (John 1:4). When we bear the fruit we were designed to bear, we glorify God. A scripture that I have come to truly appreciate is John 17:4. In this verse, Jesus shares the very powerful truth of bearing the fruit we were designed to bear or, as Jesus states it here, finishing the work God gave us to do. "I have glorified thee on the earth: I have finished the work which thou gavest me to do."

We glorify God on the earth when we do what we were designed to do; when we bear fruit where we are planted!

Warning! Take notice of what happens when we only look like we have fruit, but in reality, we do not.

Mark 11:13-14 (Verse 13)"And seeing a fig tree afar off having leaves, he came, if haply he might find any thing thereon: and when he came to it, he found nothing but leaves; for the time of figs was not yet."
(Verse 14) "And Jesus answered and said unto it, No man eat fruit of thee hereafter for ever. And his disciples heard it."

This verse used to give me fits. Why did Jesus get angry at a tree not bearing fruit when it wasn't even the time of year for figs to be on that tree in the first place? Look at it again, "for the time of figs was not yet!" After some research, I found a reason that helped me make sense of His response. The way you know a fig tree has fruit is by its leaves. When a fig tree has leaves, it is a sign it also has fruit. So even though it wasn't time for figs, this tree having leaves should have had figs, as well. I believe this tree represents many people who look like Christians outwardly but, because they are not connected to Christ, they have no fruit. I believe you and I glorify God when we do the work He gave us to do. The simplest way to find out what that work involves is to get planted into a local body of believers. We read in Ps. 92:13, "Those that be planted in the house of the LORD shall flourish in the courts of our God."

If we'll get planted in the house of God (a local church), we will flourish. The word "flourish" in this passage means to break forth as a bud, to grow, to spread, or to fly! We soar when we're planted in the local church; supplying the church with our gifts and talents, fulfilling our destiny by doing the work we were designed to accomplish! Whatever seed gets planted is the kind of plant that will grow. If it's an apple seed that gets planted, then an apple tree will be what grows. So, whatever you are, if you will get planted in the house of the Lord, a local church, you will grow up to be whatever you are!

#7) The Test of Being Mishandled: I Sam. 23:14

"And David abode in the wilderness in strong holds,and remained in a mountain in the wilderness of Ziph. And Saul sought him every day, but God delivered him not into his hand."

I don't know if you've read the story and account of King Saul's hatred for David; how Saul's insecurities lead him to the place of throwing a spear at David "twice" in an attempt to kill him. That would be bad enough but there are eleven more recorded stories in the Bible of King Saul attempting to kill David. The scripture shown above however shows an even more diabolical hatred. One that shows Saul's hatred grew so that he was seeking David's life every day! Sooner or later, all of us will have to deal with being mishandled or mistreated by leadership. It's inevitable. Why, you may ask? Because we're dealing with imperfect vessels, leaders who are not always responding to God or His voice, leaders who are moved by outside circumstances and what others have said or done instead of the Holy Spirit's prompting. Take, for example, the mishandling of Hannah by the prophet Eli.

(I Sam.1:1-17) A certain man named Elkanah had two wives. One named Hannah, and the other was named Peninnah. Hannah could not bear children but her rival (Peninnah} had lots of children and she tormented Hannah because of it to the point, the Bible says, "she was in bitterness of soul and wept sore." So Hannah, being the godly woman she was, chose to go worship God in the temple and cry out to Him for comfort. She prayed so long and so hard that she lost her voice. Even

46

that didn't prevent her from continuing to pour out her heart to God. Now about this time Eli, "the man of God," came through the temple and noticed her mouth moving but no words coming out and thought she was drunk (verses 12 and 13)! He misinterprets the situation. He doesn't miss it just a little bit; he misses it by a country mile. Not only is she not drunk, but she's also one of the godliest women Eli would come in contact with. In today's time, we would say she was at church petitioning God for a miracle. Now listen to me. The next few statements I'm going to make are essential to your future. The way Hannah responds to being mishandled and the blessing she received afterward are directly connected. If she would have responded like most people respond to being falsely accused, she could very well have missed the blessing that God had in store for her. After being accused by the man of God of being drunk her response is incredible. (Verse 15) "And Hannah answered and said, No, my lord, I am a woman of a sorrowful spirit: I have drunk neither wine nor strong drink, but have poured out my soul before the LORD."

She explains she's not drunk and, in the process of this explanation, she calls him "Lord." That's right: Lord! She didn't respond the way most of the body of Christ would have. She didn't lose respect for him or for his position as a leader. She didn't get defensive and call him names or quit the church and go to another temple to worship. She called him Lord. Now, look at Eli's response – he said, in essence, go in peace and the God of Israel grant you what you were asking Him for. What an incredible story but, even more so, the principle it reveals. When we're mistreated or mishandled, IF WE KEEP OUR

HEART RIGHT, we position ourselves to receive the promises of God for us!

David's' life as revealed in the scripture shows many of his wonderful strengths and leadership qualities, as well as weaknesses, struggles, and failures. I personally believe that one of his greatest strengths was his incredible ability to pass the test of being mishandled. I don't know of anyone in the entire Bible who took this test as often as David. And certainly, no one who passed it as often. As previously mentioned, David passed this test an unbelievable thirteen times. In every situation, David's response was never disrespectful or to seek revenge. He absolutely refused to lift his hand against his leader.

This is never clearer than when he was hiding in a cave that King Saul also ended up in. Saul has no clue that David is anywhere around, let alone within striking distance. In I Sam. 24, we read this account and, not only is King Saul vulnerable to what some people would say he rightfully deserved, David's closest confidants and fellow warriors encouraged David that it was the will of God and would fulfill what the prophet said would happen. I'm sure he was tempted to take God's will for his life "to be the next King" into his own hands and just help God out a little. Instead, David cuts a piece of the king's garment off. This, I believe, was an attempt to reveal his heart once again to King Saul. It shows unequivocally that, had he wanted to, David could have taken the king's life. He openly shares that others had encouraged him to take Saul's life.

David pleads with the king, "Harming you is not in my heart and here's the proof (holding up the piece of King Saul's garment he'd cut off)." And if that isn't demonstration enough for you to see David's heart, the scriptures say that David's heart was broken over just cutting Saul's garment (I Sam. 24:5)! This is a test most of us wouldn't have passed. King Saul has a brief moment of clarity and begins to cry. He acknowledges that David is more righteous than he and knows that he has done evil to David and David has only been good to him. He then asks that, when David becomes King, that he not cut off (kill) his seed or his name. David vows he will honor both requests.

Later, when David did become King, he honored his vow to King Saul. Now think about that for a minute. King Saul, after being evil to David, asks David to be kind to him "and his descendants" and to make sure people didn't forget his name. What audacity, what nerve, what gall. David, however, was a man of God and a man with the ability to see the bigger picture. He boldly states that the Lord will judge between King Saul's actions and his own.

This is the reality of life serving any leader; you included. Sooner or later they are going to mishandle you or misjudge a situation. Are you going to let God judge between you and the leader, or are you going to justify your carnal response? If you choose to be the better person and let God judge, and you sow good seed by responding in love and compassion, not only will you reap love and compassion when it's your day to be the bad leader, many times you will receive whatever promise of God you've been praying for! So, keep your heart right.

Chapter 4

Armourbearers and Authority

{<><><>}

A wise man once said, "The power of love will help you overcome the love of power." Authority doesn't corrupt anyone. It just has a way of revealing and exposing the corruption that lies within the hearts of men and women.

Cor. 10:8 "For though I should boast somewhat more of our authority, which the Lord hath given us for edification, and not for your destruction, I should not be ashamed."

There are so many teachings today on authority that are just not Biblical. I hesitated to even mention it in this book because there is no possible way to do justice to teaching on "authority" in a brief chapter. I will give you access to some awesome free teachings on authority at the end of the book that should help fill in the blanks. So, having said all that, let's look at some Bible basics on authority and how it applies to Pastors and their Armourbearers.

#1) Basic truth
Our authority at any level in the ministry comes from God. God is the author of whatever authority we have. You and I can help or hinder that authority by our actions, but we are not the

source of that authority. If more individuals understood this simple truth, I believe we would respond differently to those over us and to those under us. God gave us the authority we have, and He can just as easily remove that authority. In truth, we are just stewards of God's authority on this earth and that we have authority because we are under authority. The day we rebel or refuse to be under His supreme authority is the day we no longer have authority. Oh, we may still have a position or title, but that's not the same as having authority! Nehemiah had authority from God to rebuild the wall at Jerusalem, but he didn't have a great title or position. He was the king's cupbearer. This meant his job was to test the water and wine to see if it was poisoned. The cupbearer was a disposable commodity. If he died no one really cared. He was easily replaced.

Nehemiah's authority came directly from God, the God who gave him favor with his boss; enough favor to give him time off to accomplish his goal, and the king funded the whole thing! Then God gave him favor with the people so that he could convince the people that they could rebuild the wall. They recognized his authority was from God and willingly submitted and supported his mission. Titles are for accountability and responsibility while authority is for the use of those submitted to God.

#2) Basic truth
The authority God gave you was given to build people up, NOT tear them down! Notice Paul plainly states that the authority

God gave him was for their edification and not their destruction. This is fascinating to me because, for most of my life, the authorities I encountered used their authority to do nothing but tear people down. They treated people like cattle to be driven or horses to be ridden. Titles were mistaken for authority and were used to browbeat people into submission. This is the very nature of man outside of God and his divine influence. Man wants to dominate through intimidation and fear. This, however, is not the way the Kingdom of God is set up. Jesus said it this way in Matt. 20:25 - 28 (Verse 25) "But Jesus called them unto him, and said, Ye know the princes of the Gentiles exercise authority upon them."

(Verse 26) "But it shall not be so among you: but whosoever will be great among you, let him be your minister."

(Verse 27) "And whosoever will be chief among you, let him be your servant."

(Verse 28) "Even as the Son of man came not to be ministered unto, but to minister, and to give his life a ransom for many."

In the mind of God, authority was not for lording over others like an egotistical tyrant who orders people around to fulfill his every whim. Instead, God desires that we lead those He's joined us to by serving them; that our authority would be used to help people by building them up through encouragement and edification, to help them become the very best they can be and, in doing so, they would help you and I become the very best we can be. The word Paul used was "edification." Edification means: to build up, higher and higher. It's where we get the word edifice. An edifice is defined as a large, imposing building. That's the goal of all godly leaders: to build up people who become a spiritual edifice.

The Bible says we're all lively stones built up into a spiritual house. This is the church, it's a spiritual edifice. The church I'm a part of has a mission statement that says, "We build healthy Churches that grow people in Christ". This is a simplistic way of saying that we serve people by building them up and the result is a healthy edifice that we call Victory Life Church. We build them up by helping them see who they are as a new creature in Christ. We help them discover their gifts and talents. We've created healthy environments where spiritual growth is made possible. No one can make people grow, but when you create healthy environments like "worship, community, and serving opportunities," people have the best opportunities to grow. When you constantly make available the five key ingredients to spiritual maturity: The Word of God, Covenant Relationships, Serving Opportunities, Altar Experiences and Personal Disciplines, then anyone desiring and seeking growth will grow! That's the reason God gives authority; to build people up higher and higher till they become a part of God's spiritual edifice.

This doesn't mean we don't deal with sin. It means we don't use our authority to tear people down. Remember, authority is not for their destruction. The Strong's Concordance defines the word destruction as "destruction, ruin or loss: eternal loss." How many people are not in church today because someone in leadership destroyed them, ruined their idea of a loving God because of how they tore them down. When we don't use loving correction "like how we would handle a little child or our grandchildren" when handling God's people, we could lose them. God forbid that these folks don't become eternally lost; that they don't become angry at the church and God and give up on their salvation. How many people do you know who were once active members of a church and now they're not? How many got offended because someone in leadership had a "my way or the highway" attitude? It breaks my heart to hear the way people were treated in other churches; pastors literally cussing them out in their office after "preaching a message about God's love"! One man came here broken, disillusioned and was seeking to understand forgiveness because his wife ran off with his former Pastor. This man had humbled himself and went to his Pastor seeking help for his marriage. Instead of loving help and guidance for his marriage relationship, he lost his wife to the very man of God who spoke to him about faithfulness, covenant, and that adultery is wrong. This, my friends, is why I spend so much time explaining to new members that we are not like where they came from. That we are for them and not against them.

Chapter 5

Leaders Need Armourbearers

{Insight}

There are just too many Lone Ranger leaders in the church today. Leaders unwilling to delegate, unwilling to promote, unwilling to relinquish any kind of authority. Maybe they fear ministry being done less than excellent. Maybe it's pride, or the inability to see anyone's inner potential. I don't know. I do know that until a leader sees his or her need for "team," for others, that ministry is very limited in its overall ability to have any real lasting impact.

We need Armourbearers because war is hell, quite literally, when it's spiritual warfare. When it's with the devil and his demons, you're in a serious, real (yet invisible) war! We see this explained so clearly in the New Testament scripture, Eph 6:12, that states, "For we wrestle not against flesh and blood, but against principalities, against powers, against the rulers of the darkness of this world, against spiritual wickedness in high places."

I know the Christian mindset and teaching that states, "We don't have spiritual armor to protect our backs because we're not supposed to be running." The problem with that thinking is that it's incomplete and therefore incorrect. First off, I agree and believe we shouldn't be running from the battlefield or the fight, but you don't have to be running to be killed in battle. Any soldier can testify that in the heat of battle the enemy will try to circle around behind you and, if you don't have one another's back protected, you can be defeated or even mortally wounded from behind.

The second reason this mindset is incomplete is that we "do" have protection for attacks from behind. We just don't know what (or who) it is. In the Old Testament, the leader's protection was from his Armourbearer! In the New Testament, our leaders need protection from these same attacks from behind. Their protection is also an Armourbearer! The confusion is "we don't call them Armourbearers anymore." We call them associates, youth pastors, administrators, ushers, greeters, and all the other support staff and ministry servants that make the church successful. In Eph. 6:11-19, when Paul talks about putting on the whole armor of God, he mentions Armourbearers (well, sort of). What he said was that he needed people to watch and pray for him as a part of his armor. Notice verse 18 starts with the word "and." If you remember your "schoolhouse rock," a conjunction junction joins words, phrases, and clauses. So, Paul connected people praying in the spirit with the rest of the armor. Now if the apostle Paul saw the need in his spiritual armor for people watching and praying for him, maybe we should see our need for people to fill these roles, as well.

People who pray for us are extremely valuable because they also protect us from many spiritual attacks. They just do it through prayer and watching out for us. Notice with me where the Armourbearers are in the heat of battle.

Judges 9:53-54 (Verse 53) "And a certain woman cast a piece of a millstone upon Abimelech's head, and all to brake his skull."
(Verse 54) "Then he called hastily unto the young man his armourbearer, and said unto him, Draw thy sword, and slay me, that men say not of me, A woman slew him. And his young man thrust him through, and he died."

I Sam 14:13-14 (Verse 13) "And Jonathan climbed up upon his hands and upon his feet, and his armourbearer after him: and they fell before Jonathan; and his Armourbearer slew after him."
(Verse 14) "And that first slaughter, which Jonathan and his armourbearer made, was about twenty men, within as it were an half acre of land, which a yoke of oxen might plow."
I Sam 16:21, "And David came to Saul, and stood before him: and he loved him greatly; and he became his armourbearer."

I Sam 31:3-4 (Verse 3) "And the battle went sore against Saul, and the archers hit him; and he was sore wounded of the archers."
(Verse 4) "Then said Saul unto his armourbearer, Draw thy sword, and thrust me through therewith; lest these uncircumcised come and thrust me through, and abuse me.

But his armourbearer would not; for he was sore afraid. Therefore Saul took a sword, and fell upon it." In all of these scenarios, the Armourbearers were with their leaders. In the heat of battle and in life, they stood by them! Oh, for a Support Staff that would stand with their leader in the good, the bad, and the ugly; Armourbearers who genuinely care about their leader's honor, and reputation, warrior servants who will be their leader's rearguard against the brutal attacks that come from behind. This would allow the leaders to keep leading the way and blazing a trail for us towards the will of God! In the next chapter, we will discuss what and who those enemies are. For now, it's enough for us to recognize that just like the Old Testament battles, New Testament warfare is vicious and just as intense, and we need to watch for enemy attacks from behind!

Chapter 6

Enemies in the Ministry

{<><><>}

One of the most surprising realities of being in the ministry is how many enemies you'll encounter while trying to be a blessing. I could understand opposition if what we were doing was evil and mean! But people will fight you to be sick! They will get offended at offering them help; not to mention what we're really at war against, which is principalities and powers, and spiritual wickedness in high places. There are enemies of the faith that work overtime to destroy what God has destined you to do. The good news is Jesus came to destroy the works of the devil on our behalf. You're on the winning side. Stay the course!

Matt. 11:12 "And from the days of John the Baptist until now the kingdom of heaven suffereth violence, and the violent take it by force." The kingdom of God is under a violent attack and always has been. In the Old Testament, we can clearly see this in the battles and attacks on Israel from all their enemies. These battles are very brutal, bloody, vicious, and often merciless. There are times when they took all the leaders and cut off their heads, and some situations where they were instructed by God to kill every man, woman, and child; and even to kiill the animals! These battles were often fought with enemies that represented sin. God was revealing how we are to deal with sin in our life. We are to stomp it out completely and take no prisoners. That's New Testament warfare! The New Testament is full of warfare terminology.

II Cor. 10:3-4 (Verse 3) "For though we walk in the flesh, we do not war after the flesh." (Verse 4) "For the weapons of our warfare are not carnal, but mighty through God to the pulling down of strong holds."

Eph. 6:11-13 (Verse 11) "Put on the whole armour of God, that ye may be able to stand against the wiles of the devil."
(Verse 12) "For we wrestle not against flesh and blood, but against principalities, against powers, against the rulers of the darkness of this world, against spiritual wickedness in high places."
(Verse 13) "Wherefore take unto you the whole armour of God, that ye may be able to withstand in the evil day, and having done all, to stand."

These, as well as many other scriptures, confirm that we, as Christians, are in a battle and there are weapons, warfare, and merciless enemies. That's why these enemies in the Old Testament were to be dealt with in such severity. You can't be merciful with sin and expect to overcome. Sin must be overcome by its complete elimination!

The Enemies of Every Ministry

There are common enemies to every ministry. These enemies are Criticism, Murmuring and Complaining, and Accusations!

These enemies of the faith are even more vicious, brutal, and bloody than the Amorites, Jebusites, Perizzites or Philistines put together. We don't kill people with spears and swords in today's "enlightened" culture. We just rip them to shreds with our words, with our murmuring and complaining, constant criticism, and accusations.

These are enemies of the faith and they destroy lives and leave wounded hearts strewn along the pathway of our lives! These are enemies of unity and peace and they leave family members, whole congregations, business partners, marriage partners, friends and neighbors cut to pieces with a sword called "our words." The Bible says that life and death are in the power of our tongue. Just look around and one can see the death and destruction caused by the enemies of murmuring and complaining, criticism, and accusations.

This is where the armourbearer brings the greatest comfort and protection to their leaders. These enemies seldom attack the leader from a face-to-face frontal attack. They almost always start with someone going around the leader and creating strife from behind. People seldom murmur and complain to the pastor personally. Oh, no! They murmur and complain to the intercessors and mask their carnality by asking them to "pray about it." They critique the message or method of their leader to the men's group, or to the worship leader, or whoever is willing to listen. They accuse leaders of attitudes and actions that undermines trust in their leaders. In doing so, they dishonor themselves and their leadership and sow terrible seed they will reap later.

In any and all these scenarios, it is the Armourbearer's place to stop that attack. How, you may ask? You don't listen to it, and you invite them to come with you to that leader to share their concerns. This simple act often stops the attack before it goes any further. By the way, the word "concern" is often a religious term that people use for murmuring and complaining, being critical, and accusing, while sounding spiritual! In this battle against these three enemies, silence is not golden. It is spiritual death by cannibalism! Let me explain through the scriptures. Gal 5:15 reads, "But if ye bite and devour one another, take heed that ye be not consumed one of another." Whoever said, "Sticks and stones may break my bones, but words will never hurt me" lied! Words not only hurt us, they often hurt us far worse than sticks and stones. If the leaders try to deal with these enemies, it sounds defensive. It is the associates, children's church workers, and support staff's place as the leaders' rearguard to step up, speak up and stop this before it becomes lethal. A true armourbearer guards his heart against these enemies and defends his leader from the attacks of others in these areas.

These Enemies Are:

#1) Criticism

Num. 12:1-2 (Verse I) "And Miriam and Aaron spake against Moses because of the Ethiopian woman whom he had married:

for he had married an Ethiopian woman."
(Verse 2) And they said, Hath the LORD indeed spoken only by Moses? hath he not spoken also by us? And the LORD heard it."

The root cause of criticism is Jealousy and Envy. If you will be honest with yourself, when you fell into the trap of being critical of someone, the root cause was some form of jealousy and/or envy. Can you hear the critical spirit in Miriam's and Aaron's statement "hath he (God) not spoken also by us?" What made matters worse was that they didn't admit what the real issue was. He had married an Ethiopian woman (a black woman) and they didn't like it.

In just a few words, Miriam and Aaron committed every one of these sins: they murmured and complained, they were critical, and they accused their leader. What's really alarming is the next statement: "and the Lord heard it"! Now that should cause you to wince a little. It's made very clear that God hears us when we are critical of the decisions of others. He's listening when we accuse those over us. God's response to these attitudes of the heart is very quick and, quite frankly, severe. Miriam became leprous! Upon seeing this judgment, Aaron immediately begins to repent! Once again God uses the situation to show us something powerful. Leprosy is a type and shadow of the judgment of sin. Sin is its own taskmaster and punisher. God doesn't need to punish us for sin; sin brings its own punishment. Leprosy is a highly contagious disease that causes the extremities to go numb. So, when you're hurt or cut or damaged in those areas, you don't feel it because you're numb. This allows even other infections to take advantage of this lack of feeling. Murmuring and Complaining, Criticism and Accusations are just like leprosy. They are highly contagious and cause numbness in the body, allowing other spiritual diseases to get in and take advantage of us. That's how dangerous these enemies are to the body of Christ.

#2) Murmuring and Complaining
Num. 11:10-15 (Verse 10) "Then Moses heard the people weep throughout their families, every man in the door of his tent: and the anger of the LORD was kindled greatly; Moses also was displeased."
(Verse 11) "And Moses said unto the LORD, Wherefore hast thou afflicted thy servant? and wherefore have I not found favour in thy sight, that thou layest the burden of all this people upon mc?"
(Verse 12) "Have I conceived all this people? have I begotten them, that thou shouldest say unto me, Carry them in thy bosom, as a nursing father beareth the sucking child, unto the land which thou swarest unto their fathers?"
(Verse 13) "Whence should I have flesh to give unto all this people? for they weep unto me, saying, Give us flesh, that we may eat."
(Verse 14) "I am not able to bear all this people alone, because it is too heavy for me." (Verse 15) "And if thou deal thus with me, kill me, I pray thee, out of hand, if I have found favour in thy sight; and let me not see my wretchedness."

The root cause of murmuring and complaining is an unthankful heart. Pastor Moses was brought to the brink of being suicidal over all the murmuring and complaining. The constant, day after day, murmuring about everything was more than he could bear. It will be more than you can bear, as well. This unthankful attitude has caused literally thousands of leaders to leave the ministry. In Philippians 2:14, we are encouraged by God to do all things without murmurings and disputings. There's a reason for this scriptural mandate. Murmuring and complaining, fussing and fighting will wear out the leaders among us. One of the latest statistics reveals that only one out of ten ministers finish their race in the ministry and that 1,800 ministers are quitting the ministry every month. There are multiple reasons for this, but almost all of them are connected to one of these three enemies. Moses, as their leader, had been used by God to deliver them from over 400 years of slavery, and yet all Israel could do was murmur and complain. The Body of Christ is much like the children of Israel. If revival broke out in our local church and everyone was being healed, hundreds came to Christ and the manifestation of the Holy Spirit was tangible, there would still be some who would find something to complain about. They'd complain because someone parked in their normal parking space. They'd complain because no one mentioned their name from the podium or someone sat in their seat. The reason for this response is, of course, an unthankful heart.

When people respond with these kinds of attitudes, it is so

exhausting that it can absolutely wear out the leaders of God. When individuals complain about the music, the message, the order of service, the length of the service, the style of music and a hundred other things, leaders become discouraged! This is one of the reasons so many ministers fail in the ministry. These leaders have given their lives to help and serve others, only to hear the constant complaining of people who are doing nothing in the Kingdom except complaining. I am convinced that the Body of Christ has no clue how deadly these sins (criticism, murmuring & complaining, one who brings accusations), really are and the negative effects they can cause. I also believe that we are not aware of the resulting judgment for murmuring and complaining. Let me share just one scripture concerning this.

I Cor. 10:10 "Neither murmur ye, as some of them also murmured, and were destroyed of the destroyer."

That, in my humble opinion, is exactly what has happened to the multitudes of ministries all over the world. People get into the habit of murmuring and complaining about everything, allowing the enemy access to the leader to attack from behind. The result is that the destroyer comes in and destroys. He destroys relationships, unity, vision, and maybe even the destiny God purposed for that ministry. Once again, it's the Armourbearers' job to protect their leaders from these types of cowardly assaults; Armourbearers were God's answer.

Num. 11:16-17 (Verse 16) "And the LORD said unto Moses, Gather unto me seventy men of the elders of Israel, whom thou knowest to be the elders of the people, and officers over them; and bring them unto the tabernacle of the congregation, that they may stand there with thee."

(Verse 17) "And I will come down and talk with thee there: and I will take of the spirit which is upon thee, and will put it upon them; and they shall bear the burden of the people with thee, that thou bear it not thyself alone."

What a wonderful solution that not only worked for Pastor Moses but will work for any minister, any ministry, anywhere, anytime!

#3) Accusations

I Tim. 5:19 "Against an elder receive not an accusation, but before two or three witnesses."

The root cause of accusations is the devil himself. That is why it's so deadly and why God hates it so much. In the scriptures, we are told that the devil is the accuser of the brethren.

Rev. 12:9-10 says (Verse 9) "And the great dragon was cast out, that old serpent, called the Devil, and Satan, which deceiveth the whole world: he was cast out into the earth, and his angels were cast out with him."

(Verse 10) "And I heard a loud voice saying in heaven, Now is come salvation, and strength, and the kingdom of our God, and the power of his Christ: for the accuser of our brethren is cast down, which accused them before our God day and night."

Satan himself accuses us all before God day and night. So, when we accuse one another, we unknowingly are instruments of destruction used by the devil. He is so subtle and skillful at getting us to accuse one another. One of the biggest problems in ministry today is the sheer volume of accusations that go on every day all the time in all our churches. It is important that the true Armourbearers of the ministry stand against accusations aimed at their leader. We should simply not tolerate this kind of verbal assault on our leadership and our ministries.

Accusations are an attempt to discredit, and dishonor the leadership because Satan knows if he succeeds in getting us to start accusing the leaders, he wins. It happens all the time. For instance, there's a real move of God somewhere, and lives are truly being changed by the power of God. The enemy will try to stop this move of God through accusations. Here are some examples: "I heard that this minister is full of pride and you know he's getting rich with all those offerings they're receiving." These accusations often cause the people listening to them to dishonor the man or woman of God. Satan knows that we can only receive to the degree we honor the person we're trying to receive from. If the Armourbearer does not defend the leader's honor and reputation, the leader will be dishonored in the eyes of the people and the move of God will be hindered, if not completely stopped! If Jesus was hindered from doing God's will because the people He was ministering to didn't honor Him; the servant is not greater than the master. We will also be hindered because of accusations that cause the people to lose their honor for us.

Chapter 7

Process and Preparation

{Insight}

You spend your whole life becoming what you already were the instant you were conceived! In the very moment of conception, it was determined whether you'd be male or female, short or tall, blue eyes or brown. However, you've spent your whole life becoming what you already are. You've had lots of help being taught and mentored by others as to just what it meant to be you. Whatever your calling or mission in life is, God sees you as that finished person. You will spend the rest of your life becoming what God has already designed you to be!

I Sam. 16:21, "And David came to Saul, and stood before him: and he loved him greatly; and he became his Armourbearer." There is always a process of becoming something. For instance, if someone wants to become a manager, a leader, a father, or even a pastor – there's always a process involved. There was no single event that caused you to become any of these things. It was the process of many events. There are many grown people who never became what God intended them to become. We all know 40-year-old babies who never grew up! David became Saul's Armourbearer through a process. It is that process we will attempt to define. The process, however, starts with someone besides the Armourbearer. It starts with the leaders. Notice I Sam. 16:16-17, (Verse 16) "Let our Lord now command thy servants, which are before thee, to seek out a man, who is a cunning player on the harp: and it shall come to pass, when the evil spirit from God is upon thee, that he shall play with his hand, and thou shalt be well." Then, in verse 17, "And Saul said unto his servants, provide me now a man that can play well, and bring him to me."

The first step in the process of becoming an Armourbearer is that of the leader seeing his need for help! Most of the Christians I know and have talked to want to be used by God but find it difficult to be used by their leaders. There are so many leaders who have gifted people in their midst that will never fulfill their God-given role as an Armourbearer because they will never be asked. Too many leaders today are in love with power, control, and others being dependent on them

Here are some signs of power and control issues:

- They need to micromanage
- They are unwilling to delegate
- They're the only one who can hear God
- They get angry or upset when others are being honored
- They criticize the ideas of others
- They give spiritual threats like "Don't touch God's anointed"
- They submit to no one "but God"

The true leaders of God are humble and are sincerely desirous of helping others to find their place in the Kingdom. They delight in allowing others to shine and to receive praise for something done right. Saul was unable to find relief from his tormenting spirit on his own. He had to see his need for someone else! When leaders see their need for others and then ask for help, then begins the process of servants becoming Armourbearers.

The second step is: the Armourbearer must respond to the invitation to serve someone else. One of the greatest revelations I've come to know in the last ten years is the revelation of who God uses. I went through the entire Bible searching the scriptures to find the answer to one question: Who does God use? The answer is amazingly simple and incredibly profound. God uses the same kinds of people that churches use. Those who show up and seize the opportunities to serve! I've been to many workdays at many different churches and I have never seen anyone used who wasn't there! That sounds funny, I know, but it is a vital part of the "becoming an Armourbearer" process. Too many people want to be a great leader without being a great servant first. There are so many opportunities for advancement in the ministry. The problem is that most opportunities come in the form of a giant problem (pun intended). Here are a few examples of opportunities for advancement coming in the form of a problem. Samuel 5:8, "And David said on that day, Whosoever getteth up to the gutter, and smiteth the Jebusites, and the lame and the blind, that are hated of David's soul, he shall be chief and captain. Wherefore they said, The blind and the lame shall not come into the house.

Here is	Here is
The Opportunity	**The Problem**
Shall be Chief Captain	**Getting up the gutter is no small task. Then you must defeat the Jebusites.**

I Sam 17:25, "And the men of Israel said, Have ye seen this man that is come up? surely to defy Israel is he come up: and it shall be, that the man who killeth him, the king will enrich him with great riches, and will give him his daughter, and make his father's house free in Israel."

Here is	Here is
The Opportunity	**The Problem**
Become Wealthy	**Must Defeat a Real-Life Giant**
Marry into Royalty	
Never Pay Taxes Again	

Matt 14:28, "And Peter answered him and said, Lord, if it be thou, bid me come unto thee on the water."

Here is **The Opportunity**	Here is **The Problem**
Walk on Water	**Must Get Out of the Boat**

So, one of the greatest keys to anyone being used by God is showing up and seizing the opportunities that are presented to you. Opportunities like washing the hands of a prophet (Elisha), being a king's water tester (Nehemiah), or maybe being a shepherd boy (like David).

The third step in the process of becoming an armourbearer is: we must learn to love each other greatly! One of the best questions you can ask yourself before bringing someone into your staff or joining someone else's staff is this: can I love this person greatly? We are often so intent on filling the needs we have in our churches that we use the first warm-bodied individual who shows up. The scriptures, however, implore us to "know them that labour among you." (I Thess. 5:12). The word "know" used in this scripture means an intimate knowledge of. We are to know each other, to build deep covenant relationships with one another; not just a boss and employee contract. The Bible reveals the power of us truly loving one another.

John 13:34-35 (Verse 34) "A new commandment I give unto you, That ye love one another; as I have loved you, that ye also love one another."
(Verse 35) "By this shall all men know that ye are my disciples, if ye have love one to another."

For many leaders, the lack of genuine covenant relationships is hindering the move of God in their churches! God's love is not just for sinners, but for those in our natural and spiritual house! Notice I Tim. 5:8, "But if any provide not for his own, and especially for those of his own house, he hath denied the faith and is worse than an infidel." When we love and treat our neighbor better than our own family members, or talk to our spouse in a way that we would never talk to a stranger on the street, we fulfill this verse and become worse than an infidel (someone who is lost and doesn't know any better). We need the unconditional love of God to be shed abroad in our hearts; the kind of love where pastors genuinely love their members and members genuinely love their pastors, and where titles are only for the purpose of responsibility and not for entitlement. Where the God kind of love that allows us to serve and be served with no concern for race, creed or color, but a heart to see God's love glorified in and through us.

Notice with me a very familiar verse taken from I Cor., chapter 13, often called the love chapter (Verse 8), "Charity never faileth." It doesn't say love is a quick fix or that it's easy. It just says that love never fails. I believe that with all my heart, but love is still a choice and therefore is still subject to and dependent upon people choosing to love. If we are going to see God's overall plan for the church succeed, we are going to need Armourbearers and leaders that have learned to love each other greatly! We need Armourbearers who are not offended at every little thing and leaders who don't "throw spears at their staff!" I have found that King Saul tried to kill

David at least thirteen times, and yet David could not even cut King Saul's garment without feeling sorrowful and repentant in his heart. Now that's great love in action; that is the kind of love we need in the local church. I'm not saying we should let our leaders abuse us, but that we must build deep meaningful relationships that can help see us through tough times. I am saying we need to stop leaving churches every time something happens we don't like. When I look at the scriptures concerning King Saul and David and I see the words "and he loved him greatly," my initial thought is "who loves who greatly?" Does Saul love David greatly? Or does David love Saul greatly? The answer is yes! For the ministry of an armourbearer and his/her leader to be truly what God intended it to be, their love must be great and it must be mutual. This is so important because both entities are putting their lives into the hands of the other.

God put us together, but we must choose by the spirit of God to not let anything destroy what God has put together. We endeavor to keep the unity we already have in Christ. Like our marriage, we should not let anyone put asunder what God has put together (including our spiritual families!)

Chapter 8

The Heart of an Armourbearer

{<><><>}

There is nothing more important than the condition of your heart. God is much more concerned about why you do what you do than what you do. The real issue with God will always be the heart – for out of it flow all the issues or boundaries of your life. You can do all the right things for all the wrong reasons and what you did will be judged by the motives of your heart and not the actions of your hand.

1st Sam. 14:7 "And his Armourbearer said unto him, do all that is in thine heart: turn thee; behold, I am with thee according to thy heart".

This is the major difference between a hired hand and an Armourbearer. A genuine armourbearer knows the heart of their leader and they're willing to support that leader. They will support whatever is in their heart from God. There are so many ministries who are lacking servants with this kind of commitment and honoring of their leaders. The true Armourbearer's heart is to serve their leaders' vision with all their hearts. They are willing to lay down their own lives to see the kingdom of God advanced.

<u>Let's look at some aspects of a true Armourbearer's character</u>

Mighty, Valiant, People of War

The Armourbearer's heart is that of a servant warrior. All the Armourbearers were men who had been handpicked and then trained in the art of war and combat. This was so they could be trusted to protect the King in battle. We noticed this in almost all the written accounts of Armourbearers in the scriptures: Judges 9:54, I Sam. 14:7, I Sam. 16:21, I Sam. 31:4, and I Chron. 18:15. In every one of these encounters, the man in the lead had an armourbearer (a servant warrior) who was standing right next to him in the heat of the battle. That is where you will find all true Armourbearers! They have a servant's heart, but that does not mean they are wimps or cowards. No, no, no. Just the opposite is true. Notice these words describing David's character just before he was hand-picked to be King Saul's armourbearer.

I Sam 16:18 " ....that is cunning in playing, and a mighty valiant man, and a man of war, and prudent in matters, and a comely person, and the LORD is with him."

When looking for servants in your ministry, you want those people to be submissive, but you don't want them to be pushovers. If they are without backbone or Holy Ghost guts, they will not stand and stay with you in the heat of the battle.

They are concerned for the King's Honor

Judges 9:53-54 (verse 53) "And a certain woman cast a piece of a millstone upon Abimelech's head, and all to brake his skull.
54   Then he called hastily unto the young man his armourbearer, and said unto him, Draw thy sword, and slay me, that men say not of me, A woman slew him. And his young man thrust him through, and he died."

To truly understand this, we need to understand how a woman killing a man was such a dishonor. Most men get this without explanation, but for the women reading this, let me continue. In that day and time, for a king (or any man for that matter) to die at the hands of a woman was incomprehensible. Suicide would be more honorable. Kings are warriors, men of war, considered fearless leaders, and to die by a rock that was thrown by a woman was such a dishonorable death, that suicide was the better option.

The king asked his armourbearer to slay him so his honor would be protected, and his armourbearer did as he was asked. One of the greatest responsibilities of an Armourbearer is to protect the honor of their leaders. This is so vital for the move of God in ministry. Even Jesus was limited to what he could accomplish in his own country because they dishonored Him.

In Mark 6:4-6 we read, (Verse 4) "But Jesus said unto them, A prophet is not without honour, but in his own country, and among his own kin, and in his own house."
(Verse 5) "And he could there do no mighty work, save that he laid his hands upon a few sick folk, and healed them."
(Verse 6) "And he marvelled because of their unbelief. And he went round about the villages, teaching."

They just could not honor Him because they knew Him after the flesh; they knew His family and His hometown. Their inability to honor Jesus hindered His ability to do the same miracles He did for everyone else, everywhere else He ministered. Now think about this and answer a question. When have you ever been ministered to by someone you dishonored in your heart? Never! That's because when you dishonor someone in your heart, it hinders God's ability to do mighty works. So, if you want to see the mighty works of God in your church or ministry, it is so important that you and I, the modern-day Armourbearers, take protecting one another's honor seriously. In today's culture of fairness, honoring a leader is thought to be cultish, unless, of course, it's the leader teaching fairness that you honor! Honoring your leader is something more than fond thoughts you keep to yourself. Honor is something we can and should do outwardly. Notice:

Prov. 3:9 "Honour the LORD with thy substance, and with the firstfruits of all thine increase."

Honor can be given to others: Num. 27:20, "And thou shalt put some of thine honour upon him, that all the congregation of the children of Israel may be obedient."

A true Armourbearer not only honors their leader, but they also help others to honor leaders.

There is one more thing we must address concerning the honoring of the leaders. Honoring our leaders is so much easier when those leaders live life honorably! For Moses to give Joshua some of his honor, he had to have some honor to give. When leaders walk in integrity and strong moral character, it sets the stage for those who follow them to willingly give honor. When pastors stop running off with their secretaries, and leaders stop embezzling money, and youth pastors no longer use youth ministry as a stepping stone for their personal advancement, when leaders stop saying one thing in church and living something else at home - then and only then does the honoring of leaders by their staff (Armourbearers} result in God honoring those leaders and their ministries. Then we will have the honor of God and in time the honor of men!

They have a True Servant's Heart

John 13:14-17 (Verse 14) "If I then, your Lord and Master, have washed your feet; ye also ought to wash one another's feet."
(Verse 15} "For I have given you an example, that ye should do as I have done to you."
(Verse 16} "Verily, verily, I say unto you, The servant is not

greater than his lord; neither he that is sent greater than he that sent him."

(Verse 17} "If ye know these things, happy are ye if ye do them."

In the truest sense, an Armourbearer is the ultimate servant/leader. When we, from our hearts, begin serving one another because it's the example Jesus gave us, everyone wins. We need more servants who are looking for a towel instead of a title! Jesus showed us by example that being the leader does not make you exempt from serving. In fact, He taught just the opposite. Jesus taught us that to be great in the Kingdom, you must be willing to be a servant to all.

Mark 10:44-45 (Verse 44) "And whosoever of you will be the chiefest, shall be servant of all." (Verse 45} "For even the Son of man came not to be ministered unto, but to minister, and to give his life a ransom for many."

I have seen a genuine revival in the Body of Christ concerning serving. The world is desperately looking for real Christians who live a life that looks like Jesus. Most of the people I've talked to love Jesus but dislike the people at church. The reasons are many, but one of the biggest reasons is that the church and most Christians are nothing like the Jesus of the Bible. When the leaders of our churches realize that the authority they've been given by God is for edifying others, to love their team members like Jesus loved His, then maybe we can convince the world that we really care about them. When an Armourbearer serves their leader and their community wholeheartedly because they hear the call of God to serve as Jesus did, then we will see the love of God resulting in a real move of God. This sets the foundation where He is able to do mighty works and miracles in our midst.

If you're not serving as a Christian, you're not truly happy. How do I know this? Because the Bible is true, and Jesus didn't say we'd be happy if we just knew we're supposed to serve. He said we'd be happy if we knew this AND did it (John 13:17). Almost anyone who's been to church more than three times has heard something about serving. The problem is just knowing about serving is not the same as serving. It's the actual act of serving that makes a Christian happy. If you will think about every time you've served someone else selflessly, how did it make you feel? Happy! That's because the Bible is true! God's Armourbearer is a true servant from top to bottom, head to toe, through and through. Jesus was the greatest armourbearer ever because He served with the greatest heart of all. He gave His life a ransom for many and took on the form of a servant. That's what an Armourbearer does. They lay down their life and put on the form of a servant. In Philippians 2: 5-8, we are told to have the same mind that Christ had. Then we are told what that mind is; being a servant!

They Have Good Character

Gal.5:22-23 (Verse 22) "But the fruit of the Spirit is love, joy,

peace, longsuffering, gentleness, goodness, faith."
(Verse 23) "Meekness, temperance: against such there is no law."

Our personal disciplines will always find their way into our public expressions! The true Armourbearer seeks to be a person who is worthy of being followed, an example to others of how to be a warrior servant that's courageous and compassionate, one who reflects the nature of Christ. They live a life that expresses and demonstrates the fruit of the Spirit.

If our leaders are to feel confident in placing their lives and future in our hands, we must be people of great character with attributes like confidentiality, loyalty, faithfulness, being trustworthy, walking in forgiveness, having self-control, being patient, correctable and teachable, just to name a few. Remember, in Numbers 20:27, Moses was commanded by God to give Joshua some of his honor in front of the people so they would obey and follow Joshua when the time came. Remember the revelation? You can't give something you don't have! As previously mentioned, Moses had to have honor before he could give any to Joshua. The same is true about you and me. We can't give what we don't have. If we want those connected to us, "family, friends, co-laborers," to be affected in a positive way by us, we must be people of positive character. A person's gifts, talents, and callings are all gifts from the Creator, but a person's character is a personal choice! We should all seek to be individuals of such good character that the leaders we are connected to feel safe and secure with us.

They are assured in their hearts that we have their back and will support them as we know we are supported by them. My Pastor knows that I can be counted on in any given situation or circumstance to walk in integrity and faithfulness and that my word is good. If I say I will take care of it, he knows I will take care of it.

I recently heard some very popular leaders, that I have the utmost respect for, make some very derogatory comments about an Armourbearer. In essence, they said an Armourbearer was an Old Testament concept in which almost all of them desired their leader's position and had bad and harmful intentions in their hearts concerning their leaders! Now I love these leaders and wish nothing but good for them. Knowing that we all miss the mark sometimes and desiring to sow mercy so I can receive mercy, I want to say, they're wrong.

Not only is the concept wrong, but it's also completely opposite of what the scriptures teach us. They didn't wish any harm upon their leaders. They wouldn't take their leader's lives even when asked to do so! In I Sam.31:4-6, King Saul's replacement Armourbearer, the one who took David's place, was commanded by Saul to kill him, because he didn't want his enemies to capture him and torture him. They were in the heat of battle and the battle wasn't looking good for them. Saul had been seriously wounded and feared what the enemy army would do to him if he were captured. The abuse Sampson received may have come to mind. So, Saul commanded his

Armourbearer to kill him to avoid any possibility of being tortured. If his Armourbearer wanted to get rid of his king, here was the perfect opportunity! His Armourbearer just couldn't do it – he refused to do it – so King Saul took his own life! The only account of what can be perceived as an Armourbearer doing evil unto his leader is when Abimelech was struck in the head by a rock thrown from a high tower. The scripture says it crushed his skull and he commanded his Armourbearer to draw his sword and kill him. Why? So, they can't say, "a woman killed him" (Judges 9:54). As a mighty warrior and a valiant leader in that day and time, it would have been the greatest dishonor imaginable to be killed by a woman! So, the Armourbearer, being truly desirous of keeping his king's honor intact, slew his leader as commanded.

Having said all that, if (as suggested) the Armourbearer had an ulterior motive and was after anything other than protecting his king's honor, the scriptures make no mention of it. In essence, you won't find that kind of behavior from an Armourbearer anywhere! The only evil spoken of between an Armourbearer and their leader was done by a leader to his Armourbearer. It's a familiar story. King Saul attempted to kill his Armourbearer, David, at least thirteen recorded times. The scriptures also reveal that Saul sought David's life every day (I Sam. 23:14) and that David was Saul's enemy for the rest of his life (I Sam. 18:29). It's a historical and Biblical fact that it wasn't the Armourbearer who had evil intentions toward the leader but in fact, the leader who had ill intentions towards the Armourbearer.

Chapter 9

Your Personal Vision

{<><><>}

No matter how successful you become in life, you will always be serving someone else's vision: God's! God knows the plans He has for you. He is very desirous of you fulfilling that destiny. So many people will delay that destiny or possibly even miss it entirely because they can't trust God's ability to, in His timing, bring it to pass while they're serving someone else. I want you to know that everything you do is sowing to your future ministry, so I encourage you to sow good seed because "whatever you sow, you shall reap!"

Luke 16:10-12 (Verse 10) "He that is faithful in that which is least is faithful also in much: and he that is unjust in the least is unjust also in much."
(Verse 11) "If therefore ye have not been faithful in the unrighteous mammon, who will commit to your trust the true riches?"
(Verse 12) "And if ye have not been faithful in that which is another man's, who shall give you that which is your own?"

Have you been faithful with that which belongs to another

man? What a question, but your answer to that question holds a key (if not THE key) to your future. The scriptures are filled with the need for faithfulness, but no one talks about being faithful to someone else's vision/"their stuff." The scripture here uses the words "true riches" and "that which is your own" synonymously. If you're serious about succeeding in ministry, then these scriptures are very important to you.

3 Really Important Questions

1) What are the true riches?
2) What does it mean to be faithful with what belongs to another?
3) What about my vision?

What are the true riches? The very fact that Jesus used the words "true riches" means there are riches that are false riches. According to the scriptural context, the unrighteous mammon (money) is described here as false riches. If you read the story correctly, you will see that money is considered the least of things we are to be faithful with. We know that money, in and of itself, is neither good nor bad; it's neutral. Money is a test, yes, but it's the least of many tests we will face in our lives. Being faithful with our money is a small test compared to being faithful with our gifts and calling! I believe, in its simplest form, "true riches" deal with spiritual and eternal matters while "false riches" deals with carnal and temporal things; things like being famous or financially rich. These things, when we put our trust in them, once they're fulfilled or realized, leave us empty and disappointed. To me, this is what makes them "false riches." It's like the chocolate bunny you would buy at Easter that you paid way too much for and it ends up being hollow, empty and not lasting near as long as you thought it would.

When Jesus talked about true riches, He was talking about things that money can't buy, like the gifts of the Spirit, the anointing of God, the joy of the Lord, the ability to hear and obey the voice of God, the grace of God working in your life, and understanding the scriptures, for they are spiritually discerned. That would mean false riches would be things like money, houses, jobs, and even titles or positions. All these things bring temporary peace and security, but it never lasts very long. God wants with all of His heart for you to receive the true riches. You and I finding and fulfilling our destiny would be one of the true riches. To go to your grave completely empty, having done all the work God gave you to do, would be one of those true riches. Jesus said, in John 17:4, that He glorified God on the earth by finishing the work that God had given Him to do! God's desire is for us to finish the work He gave us to do; to receive the true riches, the eternal riches of the Kingdom and not the temporal imitations of this earth! I believe that one of the greatest true riches you and I will receive is to, at the end of our earthly journey, hear our Lord and Savior say, "Well done thou good and faithful servant, enter thou into the joy of thy Lord!" Oh, what a treasure that will be!!!!

What does it mean to be faithful with what belongs to another? Remember what the second question is? Are you being faithful with that which belongs to another? When you serve as an Armourbearer to a leader, you are serving another man and his vision. You may even be the senior pastor who is reaping the benefits of another man's efforts and vision. The question is, are you faithful to it? Do you work as hard as if it was yours, personally? Do you show up on time? Do you do what's been asked of you with joy and a smile? Do you serve those over you, like you want to be served? There are many reasons you should be able to say yes to all these questions. The most important reason I believe is that you love God and want to please Him. Another very important reason is that you believe the Bible is true! So, you believe "what you sow is what you reap!" This is a principle of the kingdom and, like all spiritual truths, it will work for you or against you, but it always works. You must, however, see this truth in the light of how you are to serve others. You're sowing to how people will serve you in the future. There's no escaping this truth. If you're serving in another man's ministry with passion and integrity, the principle of sowing and reaping is a beautiful thing that works for you. If, however, you're murmuring and complaining, coming in late, leaving early and creating strife with other members of the team, then that same principle of sowing and reaping becomes a curse to you. If you're guilty of the latter, stop now - right now. Repent. Turn around. Change your mind and don't do that anymore! Then you have positioned yourself where God can give you what belongs to you: the true riches of God's kingdom that are yours. So be faithful where you are and with what you've been given. That is how you are faithful with what belongs to another. You will then receive the promise of the scriptures and be given what belongs to you: the true riches of the kingdom!

Prov. 29:18 "Where there is no vision, the people perish"

Big Vision/Little Vision! The need for vision is so vital to you, to your family, to a local church, community, and even a country. Having a vision will give people a goal, a target, and a bullseye to aim for, as well as providing different forms of restraints. For instance, any person with a vision to become a long-distance runner in the Olympics knows he can't allow himself to become lazy, overweight and still make his goal come true. His vision gives him something concrete to shoot for and restrains him from any activities that will deny him his prize. All leaders need a God-given vision for whoever, whatever and wherever they've been called to lead. Not having a vision while asking people to join you is like asking someone to get on a bus without telling them where they're going. The truth is, whatever vision God has placed in your heart as a servant should fit within the larger vision of the leader(s) you're serving, a wheel within a wheel, a little vision within a big vision! The real scary part of being an Armourbearer is that of putting your future into the hands of someone else. How will God accomplish what He's placed in your heart for a vision if you're serving someone else's vision? How can you lead if you're always following? Just a little side note: the best leaders have always been great followers! What if those over you won't promote you? All these questions are legitimate questions and I will attempt to answer them. The answers, however, come initially in the form of more questions.

The first question that affects all the other questions is, "Did God call you to serve where you are?" If the answer is yes, then keep serving! The second question is, "Can you still hear God's voice?" If the answer is yes, keep serving. The third question that must be answered is, "Is God still in control"? I'll answer that one for you. Yes. So, keep serving. The last question is, "Does God need your leader or any leader for that matter to get you promoted?" The answer is No - so, keep serving! I know the last one is a tough question to answer because we are so programmed that someone in authority must say "we're ready for ministry" and then we can be promoted. What if, however, your pastor/leader was unwilling to do that? Then what? What if your leadership truly missed God? How could God get you what you need, when you need it? Great question! Let's look at some scriptures that will help us unravel the answer.

Ps 75:6-7 (Verse 6) "For promotion cometh neither from the east, nor from the west, nor from the south."
(Verse 7) "But God is the judge: he putteth down one, and setteth up another."

We must first believe God's Word; that genuine promotion doesn't come from man, but from God! Promotion may come through man, but never from a man. A man may appoint but it is God who anoints. God lifts up and God puts down, God exalts and God humbles. If you're where you know you need to be, then put your trust in God. He loves you and will not put on you more than you can handle, good or bad; look it up (I Cor.10:13)! So many people in the Kingdom of God have great hearts, but they are much like teenagers. They have all they need to be grown up and mature except the thing they need most: experience. We know as adults that it's time-tested experiences in life that make the difference in maturity and immaturity.

Like so many teenagers who believe they're ready for more responsibility, many leaders believe they're ready for more, but they are not! If you were ready for promotion, your Heavenly Father will make a way "where there seems to be no way" for you to be promoted.

What if the leader(s) over you are not hearing God, or maybe even unwilling to get you what you're in need of? Great question! Let's look at a story that should help us with this very real dilemma, but first let me explain the situation. Pastor Moses is leading his congregation through the wilderness. God has supernaturally delivered these people from a little over four hundred years of bondage. They've witnessed provision and protection from ten horrible plagues, and everyone has been healed and given gold and treasures with which to start a new life. God has provided all that they have need of every day. They have responded to God's lovingkindness and provision by murmuring and complaining, criticizing, and accusing God and Moses of bringing them out to the desert to kill them. They have done this continually without so much as one "thank you" card or appreciation dinner for Pastor Moses. So, here he is again with the people of God murmuring and complaining, this time about needing water. We need water. Why don't we have water? Pastor Moses, get us some water, blah, blah, blah! God hears the needs and cries of his people and told Moses to speak to the rock. God wasn't angry, but notice what Moses did in anger:

Num. 20:11 "And Moses lifted up his hand, and with his rod he smote the rock twice: and the water came out abundantly, and the congregation drank, and their beasts also."

Wow, that story rocks my world (pun intended) and sets me free all at the same time! Moses, the man of God, in a fit of anger, disobeyed God. He even misrepresented the heart of God because it wasn't God who was angry (it was Moses)! One of the great revelations here is that even though Moses, the leader, had truly missed God, the Lord gave the people what they were looking for and needed, in spite of the leader's unwillingness. Provision and promotion come from the Lord – we must settle this truth in our hearts. Then and only then can we truly rest in God's ability to get us what we are looking for, needing and able to handle.

In Prov. 18:16, we read, "A man's gift maketh room for him, and bringeth him before great men". Now I must ask a question, "Do you believe this or not?" The answer, for you, is found in what you do, because what you do is what you really believe! For example, you can say you believe in tithing, but if you're not tithing, you don't really believe in tithing. If you say you believe in praying, but you never pray, you don't really believe in praying, do you? If you believe, truly believe, that promotion comes from God and that your gift will make room for you, then you will serve with a glad heart and rest in God's ability to get you where He wants you to be.

Epilogue

A couple of final thoughts: Every great leader was once an Armourbearer, but not every Armourbearer will become a great leader. Promotion comes from God and not man. Be faithful to what belongs to another and God will give you what belongs to you.

Lee Armstrong

MY Purpose: To Challenge, Change and Cheer

Challenge: Your paradigms, ideas, and thoughts that hinder a great life.

Change: To believe for positive change in every area of your life.

Cheer: I want to cheer you on through

Other Books & Online Courses Available From

Author, Mentor, SpeakerLife, and Business Coach

Lee Armstrong

Free & paid online "life success" courses on subjects such as:

- 10 Proven Keys to Wholistic Life Success.

- Free Help for Pastors/Leaders - Avoiding Burnout, Dealing with conflict...

- Do You Wonder About the Future? What the Bible & current signs seem to say.

  All with FREE Video(s) and/or PDFs to get you started at:

LeeSpeaks.com

Plus, business courses (free & paid) on subjects such as:

- How to Balance Life/Family/Work

- Establishing Healthy Workplace Culture etc. - Also at: LeeSpeaks.com

Free video previews and introductions to the following books are available at: LeeSpeaks.com along with purchase links to Amazon

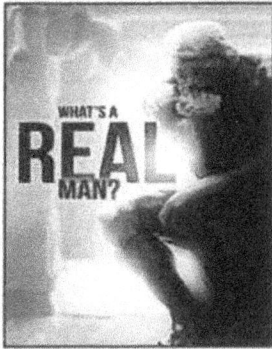

What's A Real Man?
ISBN# 978-0-616-94666-5

What is the real difference between men and women? Does a man need to wrestle bears or climb Mount Everest to be a man? In this insightful and often humorous book, the author shows what it takes to be a man!

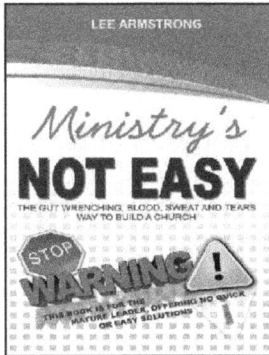

Ministry's Not Easy
ISBN# 978-1-460-98611-0

There are many books being published today that promote, "There's an easy, quick and simple way to be successful." He takes his 40 years of experience and unashamedly admits, "Ministry is not easy; it's not quick, nor is it simple.." It is, however, the most thrilling and fulfilling work you'll ever do.

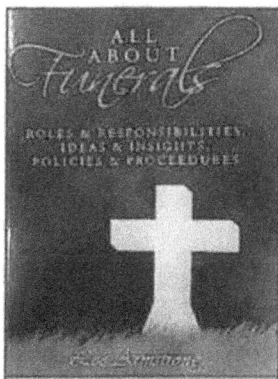

All About Funerals
ISBN# 978-1-539-05975

Pastor Lee takes his 40 years of experience of doing funerals and offers everything you need to know to do a funeral with excellence. From A-Z, this comprehensive and concise book covers it all. Roles, responsibilities, insights, and ideas - Crucial keys that will help you perform a funeral with honor and integrity. Your leadership is seldom more critical than it is during a funeral. This book will be an indispensable blueprint to guide you along the way.

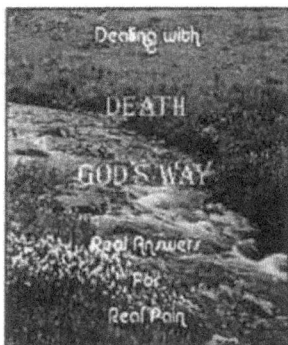

Dealing with Death God's Way
ISBN# 978-0-615-35150-6

"God didn't take your loved one!" This fundamental truth and many others are explained in Dealing with Death God's way book. The author brings his many years of ministry experience, doing as many as 40 funerals a year (including his own family members' funerals), to help people deal with their loss God's way!

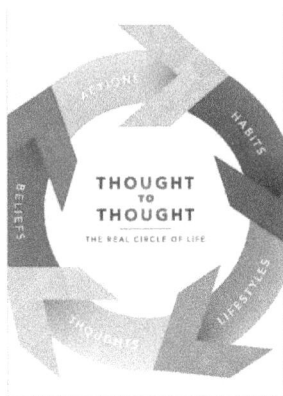

Thought to Thought
ISBN # 978-1-7326093-1-0

Everything, Everything, Everything is directly connected to and driven by your thought life. Everything begins & ends with your thought life. It's the REAL CIRCLE OF LIFE!

You will learn:
The power of your thoughts in everyday life
How you can change any habit in your life
How God speaks to you
Why changing is so difficult
Why you feel like you are going in circles
The three things that affect every decision you make.

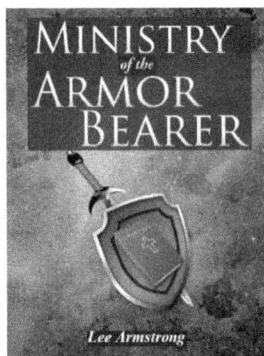

The Ministry of the Armourbearer
ISBN # 978-1-7326093-0-3

Leaders need support ministries "Armor Bearers." This teaching will help every leader and all who support the leader to understand how important each one is to the other.

For more teachings on Authority go to. **pastorduane.com**

To increase your "life success" - including greater relational happiness, increasing financial provision, clearer life purpose, and meaning, improved business culture etc. --From a man with 40 years of successful experience!

Check out our FREE Courses & More at: LeeSpeaks.com

Thank you for being an important part of our group of readers, leaders, and followers!

www.ingramcontent.com/pod-product-compliance
Lightning Source LLC
Chambersburg PA
CBHW032047040426
42449CB00007B/1020